Barb, you were right. When asked to describe in three words your years at My Place by the Sea, you immediately said: "Quite the challenge." So quick, and so you. Thanks for taking the challenge.

Contents

Chapter 4

Chapter 5

Chapter 6

Foreword

Cape Ann is a rocky peninsula that starts about 30 miles northeast of Boston and juts out into the Atlantic Ocean at the northern end of Massachusetts Bay. It includes the city of Gloucester and the towns of Essex, Manchester-by-the-Sea, Ipswich, and, at the tip, Rockport.

From Dock Square, in the center of Rockport, visitors stroll out Bearskin Neck, a picturesque thoroughfare lined with shops, galleries, and places to eat. At the end of the Neck, the very tip of the tip, on a perch overlooking the Atlantic, is My Place by the Sea.

The restaurant is in a two-story building painted in soft cream and green tones. *Phantom Gourmet* has called it "cozy, with a French farmhouse feel, and windows all around."

The décor is whimsical and romantic. There are straw baskets and small lights hanging along one wall. There are colorful paper flowers and paintings by local artists. Off the main dining room, there is a covered patio and a broad stairway leading down to a large outdoor lower deck. Upstairs is a smaller dining room, which nicely accommodates private parties and has its own deck.

From every table, there are views of Sandy Bay and the open Atlantic. As you dine, you may see a stunning sunset, a breaching whale, or me waving from my boat. We often sit on the patio or inside at table 26, from which there is a direct view of our home across Sandy Bay.

Relaxing at My Place with a glass of wine, gazing out at the sea and the people dining on the lower deck under white umbrellas, I sometimes feel like I'm on the coast of Italy or France. Then I remember that I'm at My Place in Rockport, Massachusetts, a short boat ride from my home!

The owners of this magical place are my dear friends Kathy Milbury and Barbara Stavropoulos. Barb runs the front of the house, taking reservations, greeting guests, and directing the staff. Her welcoming smile and bright eyes set the tone. You notice that she and the staff are all wearing colorful pantaloons. You know you're going to have fun!

Kathy is the chef. She is no-nonsense, with a mischievous streak, and her culinary philosophy is unpretentious. She serves fresh, sustainable food, keeping it simple and letting the plates her kitchen turns out speak for themselves.

It makes sense that the emphasis is on seafood. After all, the lobsters are being pulled from traps right in front of you. The fish, caught that morning, is coming from the docks in Gloucester, just a few miles away. And the clams, mussels, and scallops have been hand selected for My Place by Kathy's sources in neighboring towns Ipswich and Essex. If you're taking a break from seafood, there are lots of other choices, including Black Angus sirloin, lamb chops, and pizza, all from the grill. And there are wonderful seasonal salads.

Wednesday evenings in the summer, a small plane circles Sandy Bay, towing a banner that says "Guess What Day It Is!?" It's Hump Day, and My Place is transformed into a bistro, with a pub-style menu, music, and excitement.

At about 8 p.m., the DJ turns up the beat. The staff hands out colorful hats, beads, leis, and flashing sunglasses. Soon, Kathy and the staff, all in pantaloons and light-up shoes, parade through the restaurant and down the stairs to the lower deck. They start line dancing. Guests join in. Some guests also wear light-up shoes. Mine are gold. As the sun sets, the lower deck becomes the scene of a dance party.

This book provides a window into the people who make My Place such a jewel. It also includes recipes for some of Kathy's most popular dishes.

Among them is my favorite entree, the Pasta Bolognese. When I order it from Nick Hafey, Kathy and Barb's right-hand man, I simply say, "The B-word." The book also includes Marianne's favorite, the Baked Scallop, Shrimp, and Artichokes. And my go-to desserts, the Strawberry Shortcake and the warm Apple Crunch.

I've been waiting years for the publication of this book. Despite our being such good friends, Kathy steadfastly refused to tell me, or anyone else, the recipe for her heavenly delicious Herb Bread. "You'll have to wait," she would say, "for the cookbook."

Well, the recipe is finally here! With some ingredients that surprised me and may surprise you. Now we can all take a crack at Kathy's amazing Herb Bread and bring home a taste of this magical restaurant.

Ken Novack
Rockport, MA

Foreword

When you look out from the deck on Bearskin Neck, you could be at a resort anywhere in the world: the Caribbean, the Greek Isles, Bermuda.... But, NO, you are at My Place by the Sea in Rockport, Massachusetts.

With Kathy's creative genius working with local produce and Barbara's dining room management finesse, you receive a truly pleasant experience.

My wife and I have been vacationing in Rockport for over 50 years, and our family has always been welcome to dine and view the Bay of Maine from this unique vantage point.

As a Master Sommelier, I enjoy their in-depth wine list, especially the Blanc de Blancs Champagne from José Dhondt; the Alphonse Mellot La Moussiere, Sancerre 2020; and the Husch Estate Pinot Noir Anderson Valley, California 2019.

The Grilled Summer Peach Salad with mission figs, raspberries, mandarin oranges, spiced pecans, and Maytag blue cheese along with the Lobster Tacos are big favorites. Kathy's Lobster Bisque, finished with extra-virgin olive oil, is the best I have ever tasted, bar none.

I'm so glad that Kathy and Barbara are sharing their knowledge in this much-anticipated cookbook. Congratulations on 30 years of bringing joy to the "edge of the world."

See you this summer.

Roger Dagorn, Master Sommelier
Wine Director
River Café, Brooklyn, NY

Introductions

The thought of writing a cookbook had always felt daunting—the time, effort, logistics, hurdles. But everything changed when we realized we wanted to donate all the proceeds to Dana-Farber Cancer Institute and the Jimmy Fund. From that moment on, even while managing a very busy oceanfront restaurant, writing recipes and stories, and organizing this book, nothing could tire us... because every page was created to honor those who face life's challenges daily: patients, medical staff, and family members.

What once seemed like a challenge soon became an honor and a privilege—to give back to an organization that has helped so many fight their battles with courage and hope.

This is not meant to be a cookbook. It's a collection of recipes and stories meant to capture the joy of sharing good food with good people in a soulful setting. And now... you're all welcome to join us at My Place!

Thank you to Amy

We would like to thank our coauthor, Amy Allen. She has been the guiding force behind this project. We could have never accomplished what we did in such a short time without her drive, organizational skills, and patience. Thank you, Amy. Do you know that you were the first person outside of the My Place kitchen staff allowed to make the infamous Herb Bread?

"What's in this bread?" she asked.

"Nope, not until we write the cookbook!" Kath replied.

"When do you want to write the cookbook?" she asked.

"When it slows down in November..." Kath replied.

"Cookbook?..." We did it!!

—Kathy Milbury and Barbara Stavropoulos

From: Amy Allen

To: My Place by the Sea

Subject: Cookbook?

That's the email header that led to this book. Well, sort of. I first got to know Kathy, Barb, and Nick when I wrote about My Place by the Sea for my website, Palate & Palette, in May 2024. Our mutual friend and my neighbor Ken Novack has lots of insider knowledge and he helped me prep for the interview. Among the fun questions he suggested I include in my interview was one about the ingredients in their legendary Herb Bread.

Did he suggest the question in the spirit of investigative journalism or was it his creative attempt to get the recipe after years of asking for it? I'm not sure. But when I asked Kathy: Molasses, beer, and oregano? She smiled and said, "Nope. You're going to have to wait for the cookbook!"

Kathy told me she always wanted to write a book. She showed me one produced by the Friends of Dana-Farber Cancer Institute that featured two of her recipes. The cookbook highlighted recipes from top chefs in the Boston area and even included a photo of them gathered together.

Wrapping up the interview, I asked Kathy and Barb, "So when is the cookbook coming out?" They did not offer a date for what had always been on their life's to-do list. But Kathy said with enthusiasm, "Oh, we have SO many stories!" Barb added: "The things that have happened over the years, you would not believe!" I was intrigued as well as interested in the Herb Bread recipe and, therefore, spontaneously offered to help them write it. But this was in the middle of their busy summer season. They advised me to ask again in late fall when they had time to breathe.

Fast forward to November, when I sent the "Cookbook?" email. Kathy and Barb explained they wanted to create much more than a cookbook. Yes, they wanted to share recipes so their fans could reproduce their favorite dishes at home, but they also wanted to capture the heart and soul of My Place, their restaurant. And that is how the cookbook project got started with the goal of describing a special place that does so much more for people than just feed them.

In the process of collaborating with Kathy, Barb, and Nick, I also learned many things that made me a better cook. For example, dipping shrimp in a mixture of Old Bay and extra-virgin olive oil and searing it in a hot, dry pan is a quick, easy, and delicious dish (see recipe on page 77). Use high-quality chocolate, such as Valrhona, and don't think of adding less than 5 tablespoons of vanilla to Something Chocolate (Kathy can tell).

I also learned how Barb, Kathy, Nick, and their team support their community and embrace people who come to My Place and take care of them, whether they are celebrating a joyous event or struggling with loss. In the more-than-a-cookbook, they wanted to honor patrons such as Suzanne, who was ill and made a special visit to My Place because meeting Kathy was on her bucket list. There are so many others like her who came to My Place for a transcendent experience at a challenging moment or period of their lives.

Here is one of many examples of their community support. On an extremely cold March 2025 night, the water main in downtown Rockport broke. The town crew spent many hours into the early morning repairing it so that downtown residents and businesses would have running water. Simply to thank the crew, the following day Kathy and Barb sent fabulous lunches to all crew members and many more town employees.

Now, let's turn back to the Herb Bread. While we had a crew of volunteers testing recipes, I tested the Herb Bread so its recipe would remain secret until the cookbook publication date. My first attempt according to the draft recipe was too herby and lacking the airy texture of Kathy's bread. She tinkered with the recipe. Then, I baked another two loaves. My husband and I sampled the second attempt. Delicious! But would it pass muster with the chef? I brought the still-warm loaf to the restaurant so Kathy and Barb could sample it.

I will never forget Barb and Kathy's enthusiasm after tasting the bread. "You nailed it!" Kathy said, beaming with pride for me! It was her recipe, she did the hard work to perfect it, yet she was celebrating me. Barb was equally full of praise. It was a glimpse into how they treat their crew, making them feel like they are part of the magic.

—Amy Allen
  palateandpalette.substack.com

Acknowledgements

This book would not have been possible without the dedication, generosity, and support of many. We are grateful to numerous people who inspired us and helped us create this book.

To Lexie, Suzanne, Charlie T., and the many others who have graced My Place by the Sea with their presence and who remain an essential part of its heart and soul.

Judi Rotenberg, for contributing the book's cover painting, *Rockport Harbor at Sunrise*, as well as *Please God Heal Her Now*, which appears inside the book. Your works of art are so meaningful and perfect for this book and we are grateful to feature them.

Nick Hafey, our right-hand in the kitchen and front of the house, for serving as recipe scribe, noting quantities and instructions as each dish was prepared for this book. For fielding a stream of questions as well as being our technology go-to person. We cannot thank you enough for this and your friendship.

Michael Wiklund, who offered editorial support as well as guidance on the book prospectus, and who was endlessly supportive while his wife Amy Allen was head-down at the computer, racing toward the finish line.

Barbara, Nick, and the late Kindra Clineff, with contribution from Michael Wiklund, for providing the photography that captured the food and soul of My Place by the Sea in this book.

Robyn Glazer Milbury for legal guidance, establishing our 501(c)(3) nonprofit that made this book possible, and advising on many other matters along the way. Thank you for all your time. Who knew it would be so complicated!

Gail McCarthy and Amy Solov, our dedicated "word nerds," who generously proofread every word in this book multiple times and offered helpful suggestions, working nights and weekends to fast-track the book's content. Their enthusiasm and attention to detail were so impressive!

Walter Willett, Roger Dagorn, Ken Novack, Michael Rosenblatt, MD, Gail McCarthy, Lucille Saccone Giovino, Ed E. Zuker, Kathelen and Dan Amos, and Vivienne and Michael Mendelsohn for contributing heartfelt words.

Volunteer recipe testers: Janet Nally Barnes, Pat Beirne, Allyson Christopher, Jeremie J. Cronin, Rina Davis, Kathy Chen Farnham, Jody Fleit, Sandy Friede, Elizabeth Garcia, Berta Geller, Loretta Heuer, Patricia and Randy Hock, Jaqi Holland, Amy Huber, M. Alberts Malarkey, Pamela Mansell, Michelle McCauley, Linda Murphy, Chloe Peterson, Lori Quiring, Sue Small, Allison Strochlic, Marina Vasilyeva, Victoria Wallins (who also helped recruit testers), Natalie Weare, Victoria Weinstein, Wendy Weissner, Pam Whitmore, and Ali Wiklund.

To the MPBTS staff, past and present, for adhering to our philosophies of "FTJ" (finish the job), tongs and a towel, season high and season evenly, ... no "You got its," and most importantly, "You're only as good as your last performance....." We thank you all.

Dana-Farber Cancer Institute and the Jimmy Fund team for their support and collaboration.

Others who believed in this project and made it possible for our dream to come true.

The Story of My Place by the Sea

"If the Pilgrims were to rediscover the New World today, I'd suggest they skip landing at Plymouth Rock and instead sail up to the rugged shoreline of Rockport. There, they'd discover My Place by the Sea, one of the most romantic settings for a restaurant on the North Shore, a hideaway perched near the very end of scenic Bearskin Neck." —Boston Globe

Such a glowing review of My Place by the Sea would never be written in the early days of the restaurant. In fact, Kath and Barb's first meal at My Place by the Sea was unforgettable, but for all the wrong reasons.

It was nearly 30 years ago. They were day-trippers in Rockport, drawn by ocean views and the promise of fine dining at a restaurant called My Place by the Sea. Instead, they experienced what they sincerely describe as the worst meal of their lives.

The rice could have chipped a molar. The vegetables couldn't be pierced by a fork. A suspicious filmy goo topped the swordfish. And the tuna? Still frozen in the center. Dessert was lackluster, store-bought at best. It was abundantly clear that the owners were more concerned with the bottom line than the total experience of their customers. At the time, the water views were the only thing the restaurant had going for it. It took a series of unlikely events before the tourist trap would be transformed into the beloved, magical place it is today.

BARB'S UNEXPECTED PATH TO FRONT OF THE HOUSE

Barbara Stavropoulos grew up in a 38-room mansion in Maryland. Her grandfather patented the sugar ice cream cone and founded companies such as Sweetheart Plastics and the Maryland Match Company. She was a dancer, fashion runway model, and dance instructor. Unfortunately, a serious car accident ended that dynamic chapter of her life but opened a new and wonderfully different one.

WHEN THE SEED WAS PLANTED

Kathy Milbury is the youngest of seven children, five of them boys, who grew up in Walpole, Massachusetts. Becoming a chef was not her childhood dream. Her father passed away when she was 10, placing a heavy load on her mother, who worked the 3 p.m. to 11 p.m. shift as a nurse. Her mother would leave her notes, such as "put the chicken in the oven at 350." Accordingly, cooking was a necessity, not a calling.

That changed when, as a college student on her summer breaks, Kathy headed to Nantucket to work. After a couple weeks working a landscaping job, she decided it wasn't for her and chose the second-most-common Nantucket summer gig for college students: restaurant work. She joined the crew at The Boarding House, a fine-dining restaurant run by Jim Perelman. "It was an introduction to food that I am so lucky I had. Some of the things that I learned to cook during those first years in Nantucket led to the best recipes that I make today."

That first summer, she prepped salads and desserts. By the next summer, she was working on the line. She became accustomed to and comfortable with the hectic pace, working as part of a small team putting out meals. She treasured the opportunity to learn about food preparation. Kath recalls, "I loved the frenetic pace of preparing multiple meals with a team. I realized I loved cooking."

Her time on Nantucket shaped her palate and philosophy. Numerous chefs from New York and other major cities cooked there during summers, elevating the culinary sophistication of the island and making it an ideal training ground for Kathy.

Local farmers on the island delivered just-picked produce straight to the kitchen. Fishermen delivered their fresh catch: sometimes whole swordfish. She recalls they would haul it right through the dining room in front of the patrons, confirming the claim the seafood was fresh! "At 7 a.m., flounder would come in, we'd have classical music playing, and Jim would say, 'Kath, you want some fish for breakfast?' We'd flour it, pan-fry it, and that was it. It was delicious."

Despite earning a degree in business administration and economics, Kathy felt the pull of the kitchen. She considered culinary school, but every chef she consulted said, "Just keep learning from the people around you." So, she did. One summer, The Boarding House restaurant kitchen was staffed by all women, unusual at that time. She continued working in Nantucket throughout college and after graduating.

Kathy's first executive chef stint was at the Peabody Essex Museum Café in Salem, Massachusetts. Unlike some museums that have a café or a cafeteria, the Peabody Essex Museum offered fine dining lunches and jazz prix fixe dinners on Thursday evenings. The café's elegant setting included the museum's Rose Medallion china collection and an adjacent Japanese flower garden. Her cuisine caught the attention of a *Boston Globe* reviewer, who concluded the glowing review as follows: "Nary a hitch went wrong, making us true believers in Museum Café Chef Kathy Milbury."

HOW THE WORST MEAL BECAME THE BEST IDEA

The rave review drew the attention of Fred Fiumara, proprietor of the Seaward Inn in Rockport. The innkeeper wooed Kath away from Salem to Cape Ann. On her first visit to Rockport, she fell in love with the area, which felt reminiscent of Nantucket. Soon after Kathy took the job, Fred's health deteriorated due to leukemia. she recalls driving to Massachusetts General Hospital to donate platelets for Fred, who was waiting to receive a bone marrow transplant. That experience was her introduction to the struggles faced by people with cancer and the toll it took on their families and caregivers.

Sadly, Fred passed away. His family decided they wanted only family members running the business, so Kathy was out of a job. She was living in Rockport with no Plan B per se. That's when Barb intervened. She told Kath, "I know exactly where they need a chef." This was a turning point, bringing My Place by the Sea back into the picture.

Kathy returned to My Place by the Sea—but this time as the head chef. She was determined to implement her culinary sensibility of simple, good food, made with high-quality, local ingredients. "The seed was planted, and Barbara and I agreed we would never allow this beautiful location, and slice of heaven, to become a tourist trap ever again."

Barb supported the transformation, putting her keen design sensibility to work. She planted perennials that made the place a literal and figurative garden spot. Next, she turned her focus to the restaurant's ambience, designing new interior and exterior décor to match the sublime environment of the peninsula jutting out in Sandy Bay. She arranged the tables in a manner that balanced the competing sense of togetherness and intimacy. Ultimately, Barb signed on as the restaurant host and quickly assumed management of the front of house.

Within three years, Kath and Barb bought the business, but their ownership of My Place almost didn't happen. They had been leasing the business, and when negotiations to purchase it stalled, they explored other options. A restaurant in downtown Ogunquit, Maine, caught their eye, and they put down a $5,000 deposit. They even found a house on the river. But on the drive back from Ogunquit one day, Kath turned to Barb and said, "My heart is at My Place." Barb replied, "You better turn around 'cuz' your money's in Maine!" Fortunately, the Ogunquit restaurateur returned their money and wished them well. Five years later, he visited My Place and said, "Now I understand why you could never leave this place."

A few years after Kath and Barb acquired the restaurant, they bought the building. And in the years since, they have made My Place an institution.

MAKING HISTORY ALONG WITH MUSIC AND A DOSE OF FUN

Since then, it's been a 25-year whirlwind of seasonal cuisine, special events, acts of appreciation, recovery from setbacks such as fierce ocean storms, and local politics.

Kathy and Barb led the charge to overturn Rockport's "dry town" status (see "The Call Came from Town Hall," page 26). They introduced Hump Day Wednesdays (see "Hump Day," page 94). Press accolades from *The Boston Globe*, *Phantom Gourmet*, and many others flowed in. *Yankee* magazine named My Place one of the top eight restaurants in New England. Timberland named the restaurant one of the top restaurants for seaside dining in the country. *Zagat* gave the restaurant high marks. Hundreds of marriages have been proposed on the waterfront decks.

Then there are the numerous celebrity connections. After enjoying a fine meal, Kevin Bacon gave My Place a shout-out from the stage at Shalin Liu—the local performance center. Steven Spielberg, Kate Capshaw, Sandra Bullock, and Ellen DeGeneres have broken bread there. Singer Sam Smith—the inspiration for Sam Smith's World-Famous Barbecue Shrimp, page 77)—exclaimed during a Boston Garden appearance that they love coming to Boston and coming to Rockport! Sam also told *People* magazine that My Place is their favorite restaurant.

A herd of local teens have learned a work ethic, thanks to working at My Place. Usually, they started washing dishes and progressed to running food and becoming wait staff. On his 14th birthday, Nick Hafey began bussing tables. He loved the experience so much that he's one of the My Place mainstays, always smiling and remaining calm during the most chaotic summer evenings of service. He worked his way up the ranks to become the restaurant's daily operations right-hand person in both front and back of the house.

Over the years, Kathy and Barb have had plenty of visits from former employees whose first job was at the restaurant and have since gone on to build successful careers. "I'll never forget when Sugit and his buddy Mike Akers dropped by," Kath says. "As teenagers, they drove me absolutely crazy in the kitchen! But when they returned, Mike grinned and said, 'We did it! I'm a podiatrist and Sugit's a surgeon—and we learned life lessons in this kitchen.'" Fun aside: One day while Mike was sweeping the floor, Ellen DeGeneres was dining in the restaurant and she grabbed the broom out of his hands and said, "Let me help you," and began sweeping the floor!

When the COVID pandemic hit, Kath and Barb quickly pivoted. Bearskin Neck, the narrow lane leading to their restaurant, was closed to nonresidents. Nobody could get there by car for takeout, and many older and disabled patrons were not up for the walk from Dock Square, at least a five-minute walk away. Therefore, the My Place staff carried numerous preordered, boxed meals to Dock Square to meet their customers. Later, once restaurant service could resume, tables were spaced six feet apart to make diners feel comfortable. Of course, staff wore masks.

FROM CATASTROPHE TO COMMUNITY

My Place by the Sea evolved into a haven that patrons consider a place of connection, care, and quiet healing. Kath and Barb revel in the fact that it has become a sanctuary for many. They are quick to point out that this is not their doing. They believe it has been an organic development in which they have played a significant role but attribute more to the My Place community.

There are white tablecloths and an impressive wine list, sure—but the servers wear pants printed with graffiti, camouflage, or psychedelic fish. The My Place ethos is simple: Serve high-quality food and take care of people. Feed the town workers who spend the frigid winter night outdoors to fix a burst water main in Dock Square. Drop-off lunch to the shopkeepers each December to be good neighbors. Support the Gloucester and Rockport hockey teams. Train team members to be nurturing, warm, and professional, and not corporate or pretentious.

For years, My Place has been a place where healthcare workers come to recharge after long shifts. It's where people navigating illness have grasped a moment of joy. It's where families go to be comforted with a good meal during the hardest and often saddest moments of their lives. Countless people return to the restaurant with powerful food memories and as a way to celebrate and remember loved ones. Those experiences led to their decision to donate 100% of the proceeds of this book to Dana-Farber Cancer Institute and the Jimmy Fund.

One busy afternoon in the height of summer, Kath and Barb were rushing to clear tables on the lower deck. True to their "FTJ" ("Finish the Job") mantra, no task was too small or beneath them. In that moment, they looked at each other and realized: Without their dedication, the restaurant wouldn't have its powerful heart and soul.

It seems to be ironic that the worst meal they ever had would end up changing their lives. And the lives of so many others.

Chapter 1

Let's Get It Started

Drinks, Sauces, and Dressings

The Call Came from Town Hall

It was Tuesday, April 19, 2005, at 1:38 a.m. My Place by the Sea was filled with anxiety and anticipation as we waited for the final vote tally that would determine whether the sale of alcohol would become legal in Rockport. The call finally came in from an official from the town hall—YES!

Indeed, the residents voted to legalize the sale of liquor after 157 years of local prohibition. Champagne was popped, cake was cut, and the celebration began. We were ecstatic and relieved that years of hard work paid off.

HOW ROCKPORT BECAME A DRY TOWN

According to historians, it was the morning of July 8, 1856, when about 200 hatchet-wielding women stormed into Rockport shops and taverns. Their assault was not targeted toward people, but rather at the hundreds of casks, bottles, and barrels of liquor to be found. Their leader was a determined Hannah Jumper, age 75. They were fed up with the men in town squandering their money on alcohol and impoverishing their families, all to the detriment of their community. Their act of civil unrest succeeded; the sale of alcohol was banned in Rockport.

FLASH FORWARD A CENTURY AND A HALF

For many years, we faced bewildered customers who didn't understand why they couldn't order a drink with dinner; they didn't know Rockport was a dry town. By 2004—six years into operating the restaurant—we felt we had to step up and begin the fight to legalize alcohol.

We started by speaking with Peter Anderson, then president of Rockport National Bank. We chatted at the "Ham and Bean Supper" held at Brackett's restaurant after the annual holiday tree lighting ceremony. Peter suggested we speak to another resident, Peter Beacham. Through mutual friends Bill and Emily, we arranged a dinner to discuss the idea, and that's where it all began.

Next, we read everything we could find about persuading people that legalizing alcohol sales in Rockport would be beneficial for the community. A small group of folks committed to the effort held secret planning meetings at the Emerson Inn. If someone we didn't recognize walked into our "situation room,"

Hannah Jumper, from *Hannah and the Hatchet Gang*, by Eleanor Parsons, photo courtesy of Rockport, MA, library.

we'd stop the meeting until the newcomer identified themselves as a friend to our cause. Everything needed to be top-secret so that the "NO" voters couldn't infiltrate and learn about our strategy.

A PREVIOUS EFFORT TO OVERTURN THE BAN

Ours was not the first attempt to overturn the alcohol ban. A group of Rockport residents tried to change the law in 1996, but their efforts failed miserably. In fact, a group of women dressed up as Hannah Jumper and held signs at Five Corners—a traffic bottleneck where people often congregate—to wave campaign signs in protest.

Around the time of the failed attempt, Kathy was the new chef at the Seaward Inn, run by Fred Fiumara. When his health deteriorated due to leukemia, she took on daily operations of the facility in addition to kitchen responsibilities. At one point, Fred even called her from Massachusetts General Hospital as he awaited a bone marrow transplant. He told her that if the measure didn't pass, she should raise the corkage fee from $2 to $5! At the time, the sale of alcohol was banned, but not its consumption, so many people would BYOB. (Restaurants routinely charged a corkage fee for opening, pouring, glassware, etc.)

When the 1996 measure to legalize alcohol didn't pass, guests at the inn were so incensed by the $5 fee that many brought their own glassware and corkscrews to avoid paying it. A Rockport resident and *Boston Globe* writer called the inn, threatening to write about this "outrageous" fee. The writer's wife was former selectwoman Kay Murphy, one of leaders of the "NO" vote brigade.

A MEMORABLE TOWN MEETING

At the September 2004 Town Meeting, we brought the issue forth, a necessary step to get the measure onto the town election ballot the following spring. The auditorium was packed with about 1,500 people. The crowd was shocked when the first speaker stood up and said, "I am Kay Murphy, former selectwoman and the leader of opposition to alcohol in 1994...Well, I changed my mind!" The crowd erupted in a roar. We still get goose bumps thinking about that moment!

Kay's declaration was powerful and just the beginning of an outpouring of support. Next, resident Cheryl Aparo asked people: "Raise your hands if you have eaten at a Rockport restaurant in the past two weeks?" Only a small minority did! Then she asked, "Who has eaten at a Gloucester restaurant in the past two weeks?" A huge majority raised their hands. She posed an important question: "Why would we not want to support local restaurants?"

Police Chief John "Tom" McCarthy, in his dress whites, stepped up to the podium and reassured the audience that alcohol sales would have no negative impact from his standpoint. Responding to a question from a voter who voiced concern about the proposal, Chief McCarthy reassured her that the Hells Angels would not be roaring into town if voters approved the sale of alcohol at restaurants—and 20 years later that hasn't happened yet. Next, the audience heard from Leslie Asare, a shopkeeper on Bearskin Neck. She described seeing people lug coolers past her store on the way to dine at My Place. (Yes, people would often arrive at the restaurant with copious amounts of alcohol, presenting numerous safety concerns.)

At one point, a resident stood up and said, "I love Rockport restaurants. It's so romantic to bring a bottle of wine and enjoy it with someone special. It's cozy." We were seated in the front row. Kath stood up, reached into Barb's oversized handbag, and dramatically pulled out an empty magnum of wine. Kathy held it high and said, "This is the definition of dining out in Rockport!"

The room erupted. The town moderator had to shout, "Order! Order! Order!" to calm the crowd. From that moment on, we were known as "The Wine Bottle Ladies."

THE "ALARMINGLY" ACCURATE SURVEY

Once we knew the measure would be on the ballot, we got to work. We held a secret meeting at the Omni Parker House in Boston, the oldest hotel in the country. We met with the PR person for Billy Bulger (the president of the University of Massachusetts who served in the state senate for many years). The PR expert advised us to commission a political survey to learn whether the town was likely to vote in favor of the measure. It is "scary" how accurate the surveys are in predicting the actual outcome, he told us. The survey findings would indicate whether the measure had a chance to succeed or if we were wasting our time. We followed the advice.

My Place by the Sea

Martinis

My Place Blue Sky
Stoli Raspberry, Triple Sec, Blue Curacao, Fresh Citrus with a Sugared Rim

Raz Lime Rickey
Stoli Raspberry, Fresh Lime Juice, Raspberry Syrup & Chambord

Limoncello
Citrus Absolut, Limoncello, Sugared Rim and Lemon Twist

Ginger Mango
Orange Stoli, Mango Puree, Sweet Ginger and Fresh Lime

Lemon Cucumber
Effen Vodka, Muddled Cucumber & Lemon

Pomegranate
Pama Pomegranate Liqueur, Vodka, Fresh Squeezed Lemonade & Sugared Rim

Maker's Mark Manhattan
Maker's Mark Whiskey, Sweet Vermouth, Underbug Bitters

The White Night
Grey Goose Vodka, Peach Schnapps, White Cranberry, Fresh Lime & Sugared Rim

Johnny Up
Premium Gin, Ginger Ale, Sour Mix, Soda Water, Lemonade and Fresh Lime

Cocktails

Hey Guavarita
100% Agave Tequila, Guava Nectar, Cointreau, Sour Mix & Salted Rim

Strawberry Mojito
Bacardi, Strawberry Puree, Muddled Strawberry & Mint

The Adjuster
Bourbon, Pama Liqueur, Cointreau, Lime Juice & Ginger Ale

Grapefruit Gimlet
Premium Citrus Vodka, Pink Grapefruit & Rose's Lime Juice

The Big Chill
Melon Liqueur, Coconut Rum, Peach Schnapps, Orange Juice & Apple Juice

Queen Mary
Vodka, Housemade Bloody Mary Mix & Grilled Old Bay Shrimp

The Dude
Kahlua, Premium Vodka, a Splash of Espresso & Cream on Ice

Mary's Madness
Spicy Bloody Mary with Bacon Wrapped Grilled Lobster

Ken's Rat's Ass Cocktail
"A Wharf Rats Yacht Club Original
Island Rum, Cointreau, Amaretto and Fresh Lime

"Give me an EFFEN BLOODY MARY!!"
Effen Cucumber Vodka & Housemade Bloody Mary Mix

The "Blizzard of Awes" Frozen Drinks

The Bearskin Neck Decibel Sour - The Drink That *Screams Summer*
Limoncello, Premium Vodka, Peach Schnapps and Lemon Sorbet

The Wicked Nemo
Bacardi Rum, Coco Lopez, Pineapple and Orange Juice

The 2015
Strawberry, Ginger and Fresh Mint Margarita

We paid the lion's share of the $10,000 survey fee and raised the rest through resident and business contributions. The telephone survey of 400 residents found that 51% would support overturning the alcohol ban to allow full liquor service at sit-down restaurants—a slim and worrisome margin.

On voting day—April 19, 2005—the town turned out in force. We were out at Five Corners, holding signs, smiling at voters. Not everyone was so friendly. Some opponents threatened to hit us over the head with their signs. Ironically, the loudest voice against us had once worked as a dishwasher at our restaurant. This time, nobody was dressed up as Hannah Jumper.

When the call came in at 1:38 a.m., we learned that the YES vote passed by 51%! Accurate indeed.

Our Staff Field Trip to The Four Seasons

When we took over My Place in 2000, our goal was to transform the restaurant into a casual yet elegant, fine-dining destination. To do so, we knew our team needed to experience fine dining. We figured, what better way than to take a field trip to Boston's Four Seasons?

Two limos transported all 18 crew members plus the two of us into Boston. Our team was a diverse group including schoolteachers, a part-time Dunkin' Donuts manager, cooks from Brazil, and teenage bus boys. At the time, people dressed up at fine dining establishments; however, our British sous chef and a cook didn't own any clothes that would comply with the dress code. Given that discovery the day before our outing, we took them to Filene's Basement at the Northshore Mall. These two made quite the appearance entering the Four Seasons outfitted in their Filene's finery. The sous chef, with his long flowing hair and British accent, gave people the impression he was a rock star. The cook appeared prepared for a *GQ* magazine photo shoot.

Once inside the Four Seasons, we settled into a private dining room overlooking the Boston Common. The tables shimmered with place settings for each course and glimmering wine glasses for those of drinking age. Our friend Alec Riveros, then general manager of Aujourd'hui, curated a five-course meal just for us. The menu included Kobe beef as well as a cheese course, both of which were new experiences for many staff members. Alec walked us through each dish, but when our sous chef asked where the blue vein in

Stilton cheese came from, Alec was stumped. (It comes from injecting air into the cheese to activate mold spores.)

On a break from the table, our young bussers went through the hotel, collecting every possible souvenir—matches, ashtrays, anything that could fit in a pocket. We figured the Four Seasons could handle it. By the end of the evening, everyone left with the memory of an exquisite dining experience, a new perspective on hospitality, and the Four Seasons stolen swag!

My Place Blue Sky

The first drink on our first cocktail list—created right after Rockport legalized alcohol—was The Blue Sky. It celebrated the sun's reappearance after it rained for a month straight one June. The Blue Curaçao is the sky, Cointreau is the sun, white sugar on the glass rim is clouds.

2 ounces raspberry vodka

1 ounce Blue Curaçao

1 ounce sour mix

½ ounce orange Cointreau

Fresh squeeze of lemon, lime, and orange

Garnish: Granulated sugar for glass rim, orange slice

Run wedge of citrus over rim of martini glass and dip in shallow plate of sugar. Fill cocktail shaker with ice, all ingredients except garnishes, and shake until well chilled. Pour into prepared glass and garnish with orange slice.

Hey Guavarita

We created this especially for Hump Day as a play on "Hey Macarena."

3 ounces tequila

2 ounces guava nectar

1 ounce Cointreau

1 ounce sour mix

Fresh squeeze lemon, lime, and orange

Garnish: Salt and lime wedge

Dip rim of coupe glass into shallow plate of salt. Fill cocktail shaker with ice and all ingredients except garnish, shake until well chilled, and pour into prepared glass.

White Night Martini

3 ounces vodka

2 ounces peach schnapps

2 ounces white cranberry juice

Juice from 2 lime wedges

Garnish: Granulated sugar for glass rim and lime wedge

Run lime over glass rim and dip in shallow plate of sugar. Fill shaker with ice and all ingredients except garnish. Shake well, pour into prepared glass, and garnish with lime.

Ken's Rat's Ass Cocktail

It's the famous San Francisco restaurant Trader Vic's original guarded Mai Tai recipe... Compliments of the Wharf Rat's Yacht Club from across the bay. At the restaurant, we serve this cocktail in our signature rocks glass etched with the words "Rat's Ass."

1 ounce Myers's Rum

1 ounce Mount Gay Eclipse

1 ounce pineapple juice

½ ounce Cointreau

¼ ounce amaretto

Juice from half a lime

Garnish: Lime wedge and Luxardo cherry

Fill cocktail shaker with ice and all ingredients except garnishes. Shake well, pour into large rocks glass, and garnish with fresh squeeze of lime, lime wedge, and Luxardo cherry.

The Dude

This drink is named after Jeff Bridges's laid-back character in "The Big Lebowski," who spends his days bowling and drinking White Russians.

3 ounces vodka

3 ounces iced coffee

2 ounces cream or milk

1 ounce Kahlua

1 ounce Dolce Nero espresso liqueur

Optional garnish: 2 parts granulated sugar to 1 part coffee grounds for glass rim

Rim cocktail glass with orange slice and dip glass rim into sugar and coffee grounds mix, if desired. Fill cocktail shaker with ice and all ingredients, shake until well chilled, and pour into cocktail glass.

Ginger Mango Martini

3 ounces orange vodka

3 ounces mango purée

1 ½ ounces ginger syrup*

Fresh squeeze of lime

Garnish: Lime wedge

Fill cocktail shaker with ice and all ingredients except garnish. Shake well and serve in martini glass garnished with a lime.

*At the restaurant, we use equal parts ginger purée and simple syrup, but you can mix ginger preserves with water.

Adjuster

In winter 2013, a storm battered the coast and ultimately destroyed the restaurant's lower deck. This cocktail tips its hat to the insurance adjuster, who, let's just say, wasn't super helpful (if only we were missing a shingle!).

2 ounces Maker's Mark

2 ounces PAMA pomegranate liqueur

2 ounces ginger ale

½ ounce Cointreau

2 lime wedges squeeze

Fill cocktail shaker with ice and all ingredients except garnish, shake until well chilled, and pour into rocks glass.

Limoncello Martini

2 ½ ounces vodka

2 ½ ounces limoncello

2 ounces lemonade

Squeeze of fresh lemon

Garnish: Granulated sugar for glass rim and lemon slice

Dip rim of martini glass in shallow plate of sugar. Fill cocktail shaker with ice, all ingredients except garnishes, and shake until well chilled. Pour into prepared glass and garnish with lemon slice.

Raz Lime Rickey Martini

3 ounces raspberry vodka

2 ounces Chambord

Half ounce raspberry syrup, preferably Monin

Fresh-squeezed half lime

Garnish: Lime wedge

Fill cocktail shaker with ice and all ingredients except garnish, shake until well chilled, and pour into glass. Garnish with lime wedge.

2015

This was on our cocktail list under "Blizzards of Awes," a quote from the *Boston Globe* referring to the snowiest winter ever, 2015.

6 ounces puréed strawberries

3 ounces tequila

2 ounces ginger syrup*

1 ounce Cointreau

Squeeze of half a lime, or more

4-5 fresh mint leaves

3-4 cups of ice

Garnish: Salt for glass rims and lime wedge

Dip martini or coupe glasses into shallow plate of salt. Add all ingredients except garnishes to blender and mix well. Pour into prepared glasses.

*At the restaurant, we use equal parts ginger purée and simple syrup, but you can mix ginger preserves with water.

SERVES 2

Nonalcoholic Drinks

Cran Daddy

4 ounces ginger ale

4 ounces lemonade

4 ounces white cranberry juice

Squeeze of lemon

Fill wine glass with ice, layer ingredients, stir, and garnish with lemon.

Cucumber Punch

2 cucumber slices

2 lemon slices

8 ounces fresh lemonade

1 ounce apple juice

Garnish: Lemon slice

Muddle cucumber and lemon slices with ice in a shaker. Add lemonade, shake, and pour into a wine glass. Float apple juice on top and garnish with lemon slice.

Coconut Colada

4 ounces coconut milk

4 ounces Sprite

1 ounce simple syrup

Serve in wine glass with limes.

Garnish: Two lime wedges, squeezed and dropped into the drink

Staying Safe

Family members of people undergoing cancer treatment have often told us that My Place is the only restaurant they trust during that time. Because some cancer treatments suppress the immune system, patients are sometimes advised to avoid restaurants due to potential food safety risks. Matthew, for example, was undergoing cancer treatment at age 14. His parents were cautious about what and where he could eat. He became a regular and Jared became his personal server and knew the protocol every time he visited. His favorite meal... pasta and a Coconut Colada!

Herb Bread

The driving force behind this cookbook is our desire to raise money for Dana-Farber Cancer Institute and the Jimmy Fund, but a secondary reason is this bread. I'd always said that the recipe would be a secret until I published a cookbook. When I mentioned to a friend that I was writing this book, the first words out of her mouth were, "Is that bread going to be in it? I told my family I'd kill for that recipe!" That's the kind of reaction this herb bread inspires—it has a cult following. People have told us they drove for miles to come to the restaurant just for this bread!

The secret ingredients in this recipe are partly revealed in a Simon & Garfunkel song. If you guessed "Parsley, Sage, Rosemary, and Thyme," you would be mostly correct! The bread contains all those herbs except for sage.

The funny thing about this bread is that people actually squirrel it away in their purses and clothes. Sometimes diners leave a jacket behind and we find chunks of bread in the pockets! When people would bring bottles of wine in fabric bags here before we sold alcohol, we'd often see bread tucked in those bags, too. Let's just say the My Place Lost and Found has had its share of Herb Bread.

The bread traces back to Nantucket, when I lived above the restaurant where I worked. I'd come downstairs in the morning, and Jim, the restaurant's owner and chef, would be baking this fragrant, herb-packed bread that filled the place with warmth. I never made the bread at that time. But 20 years later, when we were considering alternatives to focaccia, I dug into my memory of watching Jim and then I recreated it. Since then, it's become something I gift to friends, especially when they are going through tough times and need comfort. —Kath

Starter with herbs

2 ¼ cups water

¼ cup granulated sugar

¼ cup molasses

1 ½ teaspoons kosher salt

Two ¼-ounce packages dry yeast, 4 ½ teaspoons dry yeast, or 3 tablespoons fresh cake yeast

¾ cup all-purpose flour

¼ cup dried parsley

1 teaspoon dried thyme

1 teaspoon dried rosemary

Bread

4 cups all-purpose flour, plus more for kneading

Vegetable oil spray

1. Prepare starter:
   Mix starter ingredients in a large bowl and let it sit for at least 30 minutes until bubbly.

2. Mix and knead dough:
   Add 2 cups flour to the starter and mix well. Mix in another 2 cups flour. Coat another large mixing bowl with vegetable oil spray and set aside. On a floured surface, knead dough with additional ¼ cup of flour. Dough should be sticky, but you should be able to knead it. If it is too sticky, add a tablespoon of flour and knead again.

   Place dough in oiled mixing bowl, cover with a towel, and let rest in refrigerator until dough doubles in size, at least 30 minutes, and ideally for 2 hours. If you don't have room in refrigerator, put dough in a cool place to rise.

3. Form loaves:
   Grease two 9-inch by 5-inch loaf pans with vegetable oil spray and set aside. Cut the dough in half. With each piece, flatten the dough into a disc. Fold the front and sides in as if you were making a burrito, then continue folding in dough and rolling it to remove the air. Put loaves into prepared pans. Score the tops with diagonal slats in different directions and dust with a pinch of flour. Let sit in the loaf pans to rise until they've doubled in size, 1-2 hours depending on temperature of the room.

4. Bake breads:
   Heat oven to 400 degrees. Place loaves in the oven. Bake about 40-45 minutes, rotating pans halfway through baking, until done. Breads are done when you tap them and they sound hollow but are not squishy on the sides. You can test doneness by removing one loaf and checking whether the sides are firm.

MAKES 2 LOAVES

Dough for Pizza, Focaccia, and Calzones

This is the classic dough for our Brockbuster Pizza (see recipe on page 91), as well as other pizzas, calzones, and our focaccia. You can make the dough in advance and have it ready for a quick pizza dinner or warm focaccia.

This recipe makes enough for two pizzas, ranging from 12- to 16-inches in diameter, depending on thickness, or one half-sheet pan (18 inches by 13 inches) of focaccia. You can also make calzones with any leftover dough.

Starter

¼ ounce package dry yeast (2 ¼ teaspoons yeast) or 1 scant ounce cake yeast

1 ⅛ cups tepid water

¼ teaspoon kosher salt

¾ teaspoon honey

1 tablespoon extra-virgin olive oil

1 tablespoon granulated sugar

6 tablespoons all-purpose flour

Dough

2 tablespoons extra-virgin olive oil, divided

2 cups all-purpose flour

1. Make starter:
   In large bowl, mix starter ingredients and let sit for at least 30 minutes in draft-free spot.

2. Coat another large bowl with 1 tablespoon olive oil and set aside. Add flour to starter and knead it. The dough should be slightly sticky but dry enough to handle. If it's too sticky, add a tablespoon of flour and knead it.

3. Add kneaded dough to bowl coated with olive oil. Brush top of dough with 1 tablespoon olive oil and cover with a towel. Let rest in refrigerator until dough doubles in size, at least 30 minutes, and ideally for 2 hours. If you don't have room in refrigerator, put dough in a cool place to rise.

Grilled Pizza Bread

Dough

Extra-virgin olive oil

Salt and Pepper Mix (see recipe on page 54)

1. Preheat oven to 500 degrees. On a floured board, cut dough into two pieces. Use rolling pin to form each piece into ⅛-inch-thick rounds and dust with flour.

2. Brush dough with thin coating of olive oil and sprinkle with salt and pepper. Place on grill and grill both sides until golden, about 3 minutes each side. Top with your favorite pizza toppings. Place in hot oven for 5 minutes until bubbly.

3. Note: You can grill the pizzas in advance, cool, and freeze them.

Calzones

Use leftover dough to make calzones. Fill them with grilled vegetables, cooked broccoli, zucchini, summer squash, cheese, sausage, pepperoni, or a combination.

Leftover pizza dough

Fillings of your choice

Grated Grana or other cheese

Dijon mustard

1 egg, beat with splash of water

Sesame seeds

1. Preheat oven to 400 degrees and have rimmed baking sheet ready. Cut dough into 2 ½-ounce pieces—a bit larger than golf balls—shape into balls, and set aside.

2. Chop filling ingredients into tiny pieces and add to small bowl. Add dollop of mustard and mix well.

3. Using your hands, flatten each dough ball, and roll out to $1/8$-inch thickness. Top with filling and about a tablespoon of cheese, pinch and fold in all the sides, then twist off the excess dough. Place on baking sheet and lightly brush with egg wash and sprinkle with sesame seeds. Bake until crispy and golden brown, around 12-15 minutes.

Focaccia

Makes one half-sheet pan (18 inches by 13 inches) focaccia. Baking it at high heat gives it a crispy, crunchy texture.

½ Dough recipe

4 tablespoons extra-virgin olive oil, plus more for drizzling

½ cup chopped scallions

Sea salt and pepper

1. Preheat oven to 400 degrees. Set to convection if available.

2. Coat rimmed baking sheet with olive oil. Place dough on baking sheet and flatten it using just your fingers to make indents in it, not tears, like you're playing the piano. Brush top with generous amount of olive oil. Sprinkle with scallions, sea salt, and pepper.

3. Bake until golden brown and crispy on the top, between 15 to 20 minutes. Remove from the oven and serve warm.

Roasted Red Pepper Dip

We serve this colorful dip with our focaccia and herb breads, but we also love it as a crostini topping. This recipe also is a great base for so many other dishes: Mix it with ricotta cheese for a flavorful chicken stuffing, use it as a sauce for cooked sausage, or add heavy cream for a zesty pasta sauce. We've even added tapenade to the pepper dip and baked it with Monterey Jack cheese for a hot dipping sauce—delicious!

1 12-ounce jar roasted red peppers, fully drained

½ teaspoon chopped garlic

1 teaspoon **Salt and Pepper Mix** (see recipe on page 54)

¼ cup extra-virgin olive oil

1 ¾ cups Grana or other grated cheese

In food processor, purée roasted red peppers, garlic, salt and pepper, and olive oil. Add cheese and blend well. Taste and add more salt and pepper if needed.

MAKES ABOUT 2 CUPS

Balsamic Vinaigrette

Maple Soy Vinaigrette

This recipe uses half the Balsamic Vinaigrette.

½ cup Balsamic Vinaigrette

1 ½ tablespoons maple syrup

1 tablespoon soy sauce

Whisk all ingredients together.

Makes about ¾ cup

¼ cup balsamic vinegar

½ teaspoon chopped shallots

½ teaspoon chopped garlic

1 teaspoon Dijon mustard

½ cup extra-virgin olive oil

1 teaspoon honey

⅛ teaspoon **Salt and Pepper Mix** (see recipe on page 54)

In a small mixing bowl, whisk to combine balsamic vinegar, shallots, garlic, and mustard. Slowly pour in olive oil, whisking to blend well. Add honey and salt and pepper, and mix well.

MAKES ABOUT 1 CUP

Poppyseed Vinaigrette

This vinaigrette is a variation on the signature dressing served at 204 Washington Street Restaurant in Kathy's hometown of East Walpole, Massachusetts. Chef Brad Brooks became known for it—so much so that the dressing was what established the restaurant's reputation. The restaurant has since closed, and we consider this recipe a tribute. The sweet-tart flavor and dramatic visual of the poppyseeds turn a simple salad into a special start to a meal.

1 tablespoon chopped onion

¼ cup, plus 1 tablespoon apple cider vinegar, plus more to taste

2 ¼ teaspoons Dijon mustard

½ teaspoon celery salt

½ cup vegetable oil

3 tablespoons granulated sugar

1 ½ teaspoons poppyseeds

Salt and Pepper Mix (see recipe on page 54)

1. In food processor, add onion, vinegar, mustard, and celery salt, and season with salt and pepper. Blend until smooth, then slowly add vegetable oil while blending.

2. Add sugar and poppyseeds and process until blended. Taste and adjust, adding more salt and pepper or apple cider vinegar to achieve a balance of sweet and puckery flavor.

MAKES 1 CUP

My Place Steak Sauce

When I was growing up, my mother worked the 3 to 11 p.m. shift as a nurse, and many nights we'd head to our neighborhood Chinese restaurant after she finished work. My favorite dish was Steak Kew—tender chunks of sirloin or fillet in a rich, dark brown sauce. This recipe is my attempt to capture that flavor memory. I serve it with all our steak and lamb dishes. —Kath

1 tablespoon extra-virgin olive oil

1 tablespoon minced garlic, from about 2 medium-sized cloves

1 leek, thinly sliced into rings (white and light green parts)

¼ cup plus 2 tablespoons ginger preserves

1 ½ teaspoons crushed red pepper

¼ cup dry vermouth

4 tablespoons oyster sauce

3 cups veal demi-glace* (preferred) or 6 cups veal stock

1. Heat oil in large saucepan over medium heat, add garlic and leeks, and sauté until garlic is lightly browned, about 2-3 minutes. Stir in ginger preserves and crushed red pepper and cook for another minute. Add remaining ingredients and stir well, scraping up any browned bits from the pan. Let simmer for 2 minutes to reduce slightly. If you are using veal stock, simmer a bit longer to thicken. If the sauce is too thick, add a little water

2. Taste sauce and adjust seasoning if needed. Remove from heat and let it rest for a minute before serving. Keeps 1 week in refrigerator.

*Veal demi-glace is available at specialty food markets and frozen from online specialty food shops.

SERVES 4-6

We use this sauce on all our steak dishes. We generally have Black Angus Sirloin Strip that we first rub with chopped garlic on both sides, then season with kosher salt and lots of freshly ground black pepper to create a crust on the meat as it is grilled. This crust separates our steak from all others and the sauce completes it. Remember to always let your steaks rest for at least 15 minutes.

Barbecue Sauce

Store this zesty sauce in a jar and keep it in the refrigerator so you can enjoy it with Sam Smith's World-Famous Barbecue Shrimp (page 77), Barbecue Salmon Sandwich (page 97), as well as sandwiches and grilled chicken, steak, and tofu.

3 tablespoons chopped onion

6 tablespoons apple cider vinegar

2 tablespoons Worcestershire sauce

1 tablespoon Dijon mustard

1 teaspoon Sriracha sauce

1 tablespoon honey

2 tablespoons molasses

¾ cup ketchup

In a food processor, add onion, vinegar, Worcestershire sauce, mustard, Sriracha, honey, and molasses and pulse to blend until smooth. In medium-size bowl add ketchup, then whisk in onion mixture.

MAKES 1½ CUPS

Galangal or Ginger Root Dipping Sauce

This dipping sauce accompanies the Shrimp and Vegetable Spring Rolls (see recipe on page 82) and flavors many other dishes.

½ cup soy sauce

½ cup white wine

½ cup water

½ teaspoon finely chopped garlic

½ teaspoon finely chopped shallots

¼ teaspoon crushed red pepper

1 teaspoon mirin or ginger pureé (optional)

1 ½ teaspoons (approximately) grated ginger root or galangal root, or more to taste

Add soy sauce, wine, and water to medium-size bowl and mix thoroughly. Stir in remaining ingredients. Let sit at room temperature if serving soon. Otherwise, refrigerate and remove 1 hour before serving. Keeps in refrigerator for 1 week.

MAKES ABOUT ¾ CUP SAUCE

Chipotle Mayonnaise

1 teaspoon chipotle peppers in adobo

3 cups mayonnaise (we like Kraft Extra Heavy mayonnaise, but any type will do)

Pureé chipotle peppers in food processor or in a jar using an immersion blender. Add mayonnaise and process until blended.

MAKES 3 CUPS

Salt and Pepper Mix

This is one of our favorite kitchen shortcuts. It's one part ground pepper to eight parts kosher salt. We use only fresh black peppercorns that we grind in a pepper mill or coffee grinder to be slightly coarse and not powdery. The measurements below are a suggestion—feel free to prepare a larger quantity. Because we sprinkle it on almost everything we make, we mix large batches using multiple cups of salt.

¼ cup kosher salt

1 ½ teaspoons fresh ground pepper from pepper mill or spice grinder

Combine and store in a jar. Keep on your kitchen counter to sprinkle on practically everything!

Old Bay Olive Oil Mix

1 tablespoon Old Bay seasoning

½ to 1 teaspoon crushed red pepper (amount depends on your preference for heat)

4 tablespoons extra-virgin olive oil

A couple pinches **Salt and Pepper Mix** (see recipe on page 54)

Put all ingredients into a jar and shake well. Mix will keep at room temperature for up to 1 month and longer if refrigerated. If storing in refrigerator, bring to room temperature before using.

Sun-Dried Tomato Cream Cheese

10 sun-dried tomatoes, about 2 ounces (dry, not oil packed)

1 tablespoon chopped scallions

12 ounces whipped cream cheese

Salt and Pepper Mix (see recipe on page 54)

1. Place sun-dried tomatoes in small cup with ½ cup warm water to soften. Let sit for about 20 minutes. Reserve soaking water.

2. In food processor, add sun-dried tomatoes, scallions, 2 tablespoons tomato soaking water, and a pinch salt and pepper. Pulse in food processor until puréed, then add cream cheese and blend. Add additional tomato soaking liquid as necessary to create a consistency similar to plain yogurt. Blend thoroughly until pale pink with small flecks of tomato.

MAKES ABOUT 1½ CUPS

Spiced Pecans

I created these while I was the chef at the Peabody Essex Museum, realizing the raspberry salad needed a distinctive crunch. After some experiments, I decided to use a cayenne, cumin, and sugar mix, and since then, the pecans have become a signature item. One time, we were buying a car for one of our servers, and when we mentioned we run My Place, the salesperson said, "Oh, you're the ones who make that raspberry salad with those delicious pecans!"

These pecans add a distinctive flavor and crunch to many of our seasonal salads and make a great bar snack. We make them in large batches because they are an addictive snack and seem to disappear! By quickly cooking the pecans and finishing them in a hot oven, you can give them a lightly sugared, crispy coating.

3 tablespoons unsalted butter

5 teaspoons ground cumin

Pinch cayenne

5 tablespoons granulated sugar

1 ¼ cups whole pecans (not pieces)

1. Sauté pecans:
   Preheat oven to 400 degrees. Have rimmed baking sheet ready. In wok-style pan, melt butter over medium heat. Add cumin and cayenne and sauté, stirring until aromatic, about 2 minutes. Add pecans, stir to coat with butter and spices, and remove pan from heat.

   Stir in sugar, continuing to toss pecans until they are evenly coated. Pour pecans on baking sheet, placing tightly together.

2. Bake pecans:
   Slide pan in the oven, remove after 5 minutes to toss pecans, and bake for another 3 minutes or until pecans are golden brown. Remove from oven and let pecans cool on the pan. Store in an airtight container at room temperature for up to 1 week.

MAKES 1 ¼ CUPS

My Place Tomato Sauce

We use this sauce for pizza and pasta and to flavor our Bolognese sauce. Adding crushed red pepper provides heat and a pat of butter gives it richness.

1 28-ounce can whole San Marzano tomatoes

Pinch chopped garlic

2 teaspoons granulated sugar

Pinch **Salt and Pepper Mix** (see recipe on page 54)

2 tablespoons roughly chopped fresh basil

Place tomatoes into a large bowl and use your hands to crush them into smaller pieces. Add the remaining ingredients and mix well.

MAKES ABOUT 3½ CUPS SAUCE

Pesto

Traditionally, pesto contains pine nuts, but we leave them out because so many people have allergies.

2 cups fresh basil leaves

1 teaspoon chopped garlic (from 1 medium-size clove)

½ teaspoon **Salt and Pepper Mix** (see recipe on page 54)

¾ cup extra-virgin olive oil plus 1 teaspoon

1 cup grated Pecorino cheese

1. Pulse basil, garlic, and salt and pepper in food processor until well chopped. While machine is running, slowly add olive oil. Add half the cheese, process, add the other half of the cheese, and process until well blended. Taste and add more salt and pepper if needed.

2. Transfer to storage container and pour 1 teaspoon olive oil on top. Cover with plastic wrap and refrigerate until ready to use.

MAKES ABOUT 1½ CUPS

Chapter 2

This is How We Do It

Appetizer

First Course

A Most Memorable
Fireworks Dinner

Rockport's "Illumination Night" takes place every year on the second Saturday evening in August. In the week leading up to it, many residents hang paper lanterns from porches and balconies, decorating the town. Then, on Illumination Night itself, fireworks light up the sky above Sandy Bay.

The evening is always special, but one year in particular stands out in My Place history.

Before we describe that unforgettable night, here's a little backstory: Illumination Night began thanks to a local couple, Tim and Sue Collins. They figured that because Rockport hosts a bonfire on the Fourth of July, it would be spectacular to have a fireworks show in August. They shared their dream with us, and we agreed that it was indeed a spectacular idea!

We held the event's first fundraiser, hosting an evening at the restaurant that featured a DJ, dancing on our lower deck (planting the seed for our future Hump Day event), and a raffle. The raffle's top prize was dinner for six at My Place along with colorful conversation with hockey legend and sports commentator Mike Milbury.

The fireworks became a tradition: As of 2025, Illumination Night is now in its 12th year and still entirely funded by charitable contributions. The fireworks are widely considered one of the finest displays on the Massachusetts North Shore.

My Place has one of the best—some people say hands down, the best—views of the fireworks launched at nearby Granite Pier. The fiery blossoms appear right above the restaurant.

On the afternoon of Illumination Night in 2021—one of our most heavily booked nights of the year—Barbara got a call from a sister-in-law asking if we could accommodate a last-minute party of four. A mother and her three daughters were in town and hoped to share a special evening.

And here's the detail that made us emotional: Their youngest daughter, Lexie, was undergoing cancer treatment. One of her sisters, a manager at the Four Seasons in London, was flying out the next morning. Clearly, this needed to be a very special night for them.

Barbara worked her magic and was able to accommodate them on our upper deck, seated by themselves. We knew that from this vantage point, the fireworks would feel as though they were a show put on just for our guests. From that table, it feels like you are up in the sky with the sparkles. It is ethereal!

The girls enjoyed dinner and drinks before the display and were thrilled with their front-row, exclusive seats, so much so that when the show began, they called their dad and Lexie's boyfriend—who were also in town—to join them on the upper deck to enjoy the show. They raced in to view a good portion of the spectacle.

We could see this was a very special evening for them at a time when they were facing uncertainties. Watching them as a family, enjoying their moment with Lexie, who was wearing a bandana, a sign of what she was enduring, was incredibly moving. We decided we didn't want to charge them for their evening. Something more meaningful was taking place that was bigger than serving a dinner and beyond our control. We opened champagne and toasted them.

We made our way through the restaurant and across the lower deck, serving champagne to all our guests. Essentially moved beyond words, we then asked a former employee-turned-English teacher and her popular mailman husband if they would announce to all the restaurant guests that dinner for all was complimentary from My Place by the Sea. We knew it was the right thing to do. Our guests were shocked. None of them had ever experienced anything like this before.

We shed tears with Lexie and her family as they thanked us and left. It was very special indeed.

After that night, we didn't hear from them. We often thought about them and hoped they were all doing well.

Then, in April 2025, a party of six made a dinner reservation. At the end of their dinner, they asked to speak to us. We gathered in front of the kitchen where a gentleman was waiting for us. He said, "You probably don't remember me, but you accommodated my wife and family in 2021 for the fireworks on the upper deck." Then we realized who he was.

He continued, "We never thanked you properly for that night when we brought our daughter, who was diagnosed with cancer and wore a bandana. We wanted to thank you in person." He motioned to his side and said, "and Lexie is right here."

We looked over to see a beautiful girl with long, dark hair. It was Lexie, now 27 years young, living life in New York City, and cancer free. We announced to her, "We're writing a cookbook, and you're going to be a star in it!"

Clam Chowder for a Crowd

This is another recipe that goes back to Kath's early days of cooking on Nantucket. Loaded with smoky bacon, tender clams, sweet onions, and hearty potatoes, this recipe is a celebration of the region's seafood heritage. The chowder base develops even deeper flavor when made a day ahead, ensuring that by the time you ladle it into bowls and finish with melted butter and a dash of paprika, you've got the kind of soul-warming chowder that defines coastal New England cooking. When we begin cooking the bacon and the onion, the aroma seems to fill all of Bearskin Neck!

If you like a thinner chowder, use slightly less of the slurry and add more milk.

1 cup diced thick-cut applewood smoked bacon (about half a package)

1 cup diced onion

1 pound chopped clams, canned or fresh from a fishmonger

24 ounces clam juice

1 ½ cups small cubes Idaho baking potatoes, peeled

1 ½ cups all-purpose flour

1 cup whole milk, plus more to bring chowder to desired consistency

Salt and Pepper Mix (see recipe on page 54)

Garnishes: Melted unsalted butter and paprika

1. Make chowder base (ideally the day before you plan to serve the chowder):
   In large pot over medium-high heat, brown bacon and add pinches of salt and pepper. Add onion and sauté until translucent, stirring frequently. Add generous pinches of salt and pepper. Stir in clams and clam juice and bring to a boil. Add potatoes, stir, add generous pinches of salt and pepper, bring to a boil, then simmer until potatoes are fork tender.

   While potatoes cook, mix slurry: In small bowl, combine 1 ½ cups of tepid water with flour. Whisk to blend and remove any lumps. Once potatoes are fork tender, turn heat up, pour in slurry, stirring constantly. Add generous pinches of salt and pepper. Bring to a boil, continue stirring, and let boil about 4-5 minutes until it's thick enough that a spoon will stand upright for a couple seconds. Let chowder base cool and refrigerate overnight.

2. Finish preparing chowder:
   In large pot, combine chowder base with 1 cup milk over medium heat. If chowder is too thick, add additional milk, 1 tablespoon at a time until it reaches desired consistency. Taste and add salt and pepper if needed.

3. Serve chowder:
   Divide into bowls and top each with melted butter and sprinkle of paprika.

SERVES 8-10

Chilled Cucumber Dill Soup

Cool, creamy, and refreshing, this chilled soup is elegant and so simple to prepare. Lightly sautéed cucumbers and onions are blended with fresh dill and broth, then chilled. Cream adds velvety richness while keeping the soup bright and herbaceous. Ideal for a make-ahead starter on a hot day, it's finished with crisp cucumber slices and dill sprigs.

2 tablespoons extra-virgin olive oil

3 large cucumbers, peeled, cut in half lengthwise, seeds scooped out with a spoon, and cut into ¼-inch slices; set aside a few slices for garnishing

1 cup diced onion

2 tablespoons chopped fresh dill, plus extra sprigs for garnish

3 cups chicken or vegetable broth

1 ½ cups heavy cream

Salt and Pepper Mix (see recipe on page 54)

1. In a large saucepan over medium heat, warm olive oil and sauté cucumbers and onion about 7 minutes. Add dill and chicken broth and simmer for 15 minutes or until onions and cucumbers are soft. Season with salt and pepper.

2. Using a handheld immersion blender or standard blender, blend soup, leaving some pieces of cucumber. Transfer to container and refrigerate for a few hours or overnight.

3. When ready to serve, stir in cream, taste, and add more salt and pepper if needed. Divide soup in bowls and top with a garnish of dill sprigs and reserved cucumber slices.

SERVES 4-6 (MAKES 6-7 CUPS)

Pan-Roasted Garlic Potato Soup

This comforting soup is a great use of leftover mashed potatoes. Letting the mashed potatoes rest overnight in the refrigerator deepens the flavors.

Mashed potatoes

7-8 medium-sized Russet potatoes, peeled and quartered (about 4 pounds)

1 ¼ cups milk (whole milk preferred, but any milk will work)

½ stick unsalted butter

Soup

1 ½ teaspoons extra-virgin olive oil

1 ½ teaspoons chopped garlic

1 ½ cups chicken or vegetable broth

¾ cup milk

Salt and Pepper Mix (see recipe on page 54)

Garnishes: Chopped chives or **chive oil** (see recipe below), sour cream, diced heirloom tomato, or bacon bits

1. Put potatoes in a large pot, cover with water, and boil until you can easily pierce them with a fork. Drain water, add milk and butter, and mash with a masher or large fork. Season with salt and pepper and refrigerate overnight. Alternatively, you can use about 5 cups leftover mashed potatoes.

2. In large pot, heat olive oil and brown garlic over medium heat, stirring frequently, for about 2 minutes. Add broth, mashed potatoes, and milk and simmer until hot. Season with salt and pepper. Stir until well blended. Garnish each bowl with chopped chives or chive oil to serve.

Chive oil (optional)

1 cup extra-virgin olive oil

½ cup roughly chopped chives

Blend in food processor just until pureéd. Avoid overblending, which will reduce the vibrancy of the emerald green color.

SERVES 4-5 AS A FIRST COURSE

Caesar Salad

Our take on this classic salad has a "pucker," differentiating it from the ubiquitous version most people are familiar with. The dressing's subtle tang, contrasting with crispy lettuce and crunchy croutons, make this a highly craveable dish. We love dipping our Herb Bread into the dressing, and you will too!

1-2 slices day-old bread (we love making croutons with the **Herb Bread**; see recipe on page 44)

1 tablespoon extra-virgin olive oil or melted unsalted butter

¾ cup **Caesar Salad Dressing** (see recipe at right)

5 cups romaine lettuce, washed and torn, from 1-2 heads of lettuce

Kosher salt and freshly ground black pepper

1. Make croutons:
   Preheat oven to 375 degrees. Cut bread into ¾-inch cubes, enough to fill 1 heaping cup. In a medium bowl, add olive oil or butter and season lightly with salt and pepper. Add bread cubes and toss until evenly coated. Spread onto baking sheet in a single layer and bake 10–15 minutes, tossing at 5-minute intervals until golden brown and crispy. Remove from oven and let cool. Store leftovers in an airtight container for up to 1 week.

2. While croutons are baking, make salad dressing.

3. Assemble salad:
   In large salad bowl, add large spoonful of dressing and top with lettuce. Toss to combine, adding more dressing a spoonful at a time, and finish with shaved cheese. Add croutons and a few cranks of freshly ground pepper and toss to coat. Serve immediately.

MAKES 4 GENEROUS FIRST-COURSE SERVINGS

Caesar Salad Dressing

The egg adds a rich flavor and creamy texture that elevates this salad to a new level of deliciousness, but if you prefer to omit it, you can replace it with 1 tablespoon of mayonnaise.

1 small egg (or use half a large egg, beaten, about 2 tablespoons)

1 tablespoon Dijon mustard

2 teaspoons fresh lime juice

1 tablespoon finely chopped yellow onion

1 tablespoon apple cider vinegar

½ anchovy (or whole anchovy for more umami)

½ teaspoon finely chopped garlic, about one small clove

Dash Worcestershire sauce

⅓ cup vegetable oil

¾ cup grated Grana Padano or Parmesan cheese

Freshly ground black pepper

Kosher salt to taste

1. In food processor or blender, combine egg, Dijon mustard, lime juice, onion, vinegar, anchovy, garlic, Worcestershire sauce, and pinch of salt and pepper, and purée. Once puréed, slowly drizzle in oil and blend until mixture thickens.

2. Stop blending, add several cranks of black pepper and grated cheese. Pulse to combine until creamy and smooth. Taste and add more pepper or salt if needed.

3. Refrigerate any remaining dressing in a covered container. Stir in small amounts of warm water to bring it back to its original consistency before using.

MAKES ABOUT 1 CUP

Vegetarian Chili

This hearty chili has been a longtime favorite at My Place, loved by vegetarians and meat-eaters alike. Packed with colorful bell peppers, tender kidney beans, and a medley of spices, it's simmered low and slow for rich, smoky flavor with just the right amount of heat.

At the restaurant, we finish it with melted Monterey Jack cheese and serve it with crisp corn tortilla chips for dipping. Do not be intimidated by what looks like a long list of ingredients! The recipe comes together quickly.

2 tablespoons extra-virgin olive oil

1 small clove garlic, chopped, about ½ teaspoon

2 cups chopped onion

1 ⅓ cups julienned red bell pepper cut into ⅛- or ¼-inch wide strips

1 ⅓ cups julienned orange bell pepper cut into ⅛- or ¼-inch wide strips

1 ⅓ cups julienned yellow bell pepper cut into ⅛- or ¼-inch wide strips

1 tablespoon dried oregano

⅛ teaspoon cayenne

1 teaspoon paprika

1 teaspoon chili powder

1 teaspoon **Salt and Pepper Mix** (see recipe on page 54)

3 slices jalapeño (optional; omit if you prefer less heat)

½ cup (4 ounces) beer (nonalcoholic beer is fine)

2 15.5-ounce cans kidney beans, rinsed and drained

3 cups **My Place Tomato Sauce** (see recipe on page 57) or 1 28-ounce can diced tomatoes (we like San Marzano)

1 tablespoon granulated sugar

2 cups grated Monterey Jack cheese (avoid using orange cheese)

Corn tortilla chips, freshly made if possible

1. Prepare chili:
   Heat olive oil in large skillet over medium-high heat. Add garlic, shake pan to spread the garlic, add onion and peppers, and reduce heat to medium. Add oregano, cayenne, paprika, chili powder, and salt and pepper, and mix well. Cook until vegetables have wilted, about 5 minutes, then stir in jalapeño and beer. Add beans, tomato sauce, and sugar, and reduce heat to a low simmer for 30 minutes. Taste and add more salt and pepper if needed.

2. Serve chili:
   At the restaurant, we divide the chili into oven-safe bowls, sprinkle with Monterey Jack cheese, and bake in the oven until the cheese is golden brown.

   Then we place the hot bowls onto plates and serve with freshly made corn tortilla chips. If you don't have oven-safe bowls or have concerns about serving the chili in very hot bowls, simply divide the chili into bowls, sprinkle with cheese, and serve with corn tortilla chips.

SERVES 4-6 (MAKES 6-8 CUPS)

We've been known to mix some of our Bolognese with our chili to create "Nacho Deluxe," with crisp tortilla chips, chiffonade of romaine lettuce, jalapeño, and onion with melted Monterey Jack cheese. Alternatively, you can leave the Bolognese out and enjoy vegetarian nachos.

Raspberry Orange Salad

Sweet, juicy oranges play against tart, fresh raspberries, crisp lettuces, and our highly craveable Spiced Pecans that bring just the right crunch. The homemade vinaigrette is bright, fruity, and lightly sweet. Top it with Maytag blue cheese, feta, or even grilled chicken or seafood, and you've got a salad that feels special enough for company yet simple enough for a weeknight dinner.

Raspberry Vinaigrette (see recipe below)

8 ounces mixed lettuces (about 6 cups)

2 fresh Sumo oranges or other fresh, sweet-tasting oranges, cut into slices, or canned mandarin orange segments

4 ounces (about ½ cup) **Spiced Pecans** (see recipe on page 56)

6 ounces or 1 pint fresh raspberries

Optional toppings: Maytag blue cheese, feta, grilled chicken, or grilled seafood

1. Make Raspberry Vinaigrette and set aside.
2. Assemble salads:
   Divide lettuce onto plates and top with orange slices, pecans, and raspberries. Drizzle each with 1-2 tablespoons of dressing. Alternatively, toss the lettuce and dressing—start with 2 tablespoons and add more if needed—in a large bowl and then divide it onto the plates and add the toppings.

SERVES 4

Raspberry Vinaigrette

6 tablespoons raspberry vinegar (you can substitute red wine vinegar)

6 tablespoons thawed frozen raspberries, with juice

¾ teaspoon chopped shallots

6 tablespoons vegetable oil

5 tablespoons sugar

1 tablespoon honey

¼ teaspoon salt

¼ teaspoon pepper

In a small bowl, use handheld whisk to mix vinegar, raspberries and juice, and shallots. Do not prepare this in a blender; doing so produces an unappetizing, melted raspberry sherbet-like liquid! Whisk in oil as you add it to the bowl. Whisk in sugar, honey, salt, and pepper. Taste and add more salt and pepper if needed.

MAKES ABOUT 1 ½ CUPS

Grilled Summer Peach Salad

Peaches are one of our favorite fruits of summer, and the ones from Dickey Farms in Musella, Georgia, are in a league of their own. They're the size of softballs, bursting with juice, intensely sweet, and beautifully fragrant. When Kathelen and Dan Amos send us a box, it's a cause for celebration at the restaurant. While we love to eat them just as they are, we also like incorporating them into this salad.

We slice the peaches in half and dip them in peach schnapps (optional), and then we put them on the grill, where the heat caramelizes their sugars and deepens their natural sweetness. It's pure summer on a plate.

To balance that sweetness, we pair the fruit with Maytag blue cheese. I was inspired by a salad with creamy French blue cheese that I enjoyed at a pizzeria along the road from Avignon to Aix-en-Provence. (Fun fact: the Maytag Blue Cheese company was founded by the grandsons of the man who started the Maytag appliance empire.) We often add mandarin oranges, Mission figs, and raspberries to this salad.—Kathy

4 tablespoons **Spiced Pecans** (see recipe on page 56)

4 peaches (if peaches are jumbo-sized, use 2)

1 tablespoon peach schnapps (optional, but recommended)

8 ounces salad greens

1 Sumo or mandarin orange, peeled, with top, bottom and sides trimmed and cut into segments so you see the bright color of the orange

16 raspberries

4 tablespoons crumbled blue cheese such as Maytag or Great Hill (optional)

2 tablespoons extra-virgin olive oil

2 tablespoons aged balsamic vinegar

Sea salt and pepper

1. Make the Spiced Pecans.

2. Grill peaches:
   Cut peaches in half and remove pits. Dip each half in peach schnapps. Grill peach for about 2 ½ minutes, face down. If broiling, place the peaches cut side up on a foil-lined baking sheet and broil until lightly charred. Let cool.

3. Plate salad:
   Divide salad greens among four plates. Top with the fruit, spiced pecans, and blue cheese if desired. Drizzle with olive oil and balsamic vinegar and finish with sea salt and pepper.

SERVES 4 AS AN APPETIZER

Harvest Fruit Salad

In place of the peaches, use 1 large Anjou pear, cut in half with seeds and core removed, and 8 fresh figs halved (use dried figs if fresh are not available).

Use triple sec or pear liqueur instead of peach schnapps.

To grill fruit: Dip pear and figs in triple sec or pear liqueur, if using. Grill with cut side down for a few minutes. If you don't have a grill, line a baking sheet with foil, place fruit cut side facing up, and broil until fruit is lightly charred. You also can cook fruit a la plancha style, heating a cast iron pan over high heat, and briefly searing both sides. Transfer fruit to a plate to cool. Slice the pears before serving.

Our first visit to My Place by the Sea occurred during our first summer on Cape Ann, and it has been our favorite ever since. It is unique for its magical sunsets and divine food, but most importantly, the warmth and joyful charm extended by Barbara and Kathy from the moment we cross the threshold is unmatched. Their love for what they do and their obvious delight in sharing it with their guests has made us feel like family.

—Kathelen and Dan Amos

Curried Crab Salad

This curried crab salad hits all the right notes—sweet, spicy, creamy, and bright. It's one of those simple recipes that feels special, whether you're serving it for a make-ahead lunch or a light summer dinner outside. The sweet chunks of mango play beautifully off the gentle heat of the curry, while creamy avocado and tender crab bring richness and balance. Be sure to gently mix the crab so it remains in large chunks.

8 ounces fresh all-leg crab meat, preferably Maine peekytoe or Jonah crab

1 cup diced ripe but firm mango, plus 8 thin mango slices for garnish

4 tablespoons finely diced celery

1 tablespoon plus 1 teaspoon Madras curry powder

3 tablespoons mayonnaise

2 slightly soft avocados

2 cups salad greens

1 cup halved cherry tomatoes, preferably heirloom

Juice from half a lemon

2 tablespoons extra-virgin olive oil, plus more for drizzling

Sea salt

1. Mix crab salad:
   Put crab in medium bowl and sift through to remove any shells. Add diced mango, celery, curry powder, and mayonnaise and toss carefully with a spoon to keep the crab meat in chunks. The salad should be delicate while holding together, but not as creamy as tuna salad. If the salad does not stay together, gently add more mayonnaise, about ½ teaspoon at a time (you want to use enough mayonnaise to hold the salad together but not mask the crab flavor).

2. Prep avocados:
   Cut both avocados in half, remove the pits, and use a spoon to scoop the halves out of the skin, keeping the avocado halves intact. Place each half with the rounded part facing up and use a knife to trim the rounded part so it will sit flat when you turn it over. Save the trimmed bottoms to use as garnishes.

3. Plate salad:
   Dress small side salad of greens and tomatoes with lemon juice, olive oil, and a sprinkle of sea salt and divide onto four plates, placing the salad on the side of the plate.

   Place avocados in the center of each plate, with flat side touching the plate, and fill each with one quarter of the crab salad. Garnish with the trimmed avocado slices and mango slices. Finish with a drizzle of olive oil and sea salt.

MAKES 4 APPETIZER SALADS

Harry's Birthday Champagne Toast

Many years ago on an early fall evening, Harry Hintlian and his wife Mary were quietly celebrating his birthday at the restaurant. Harry and Mary, who owned Superior Nut Company, were regulars. Sculptor John Raimondi was sitting at a table nearby when he overheard that it was Harry's birthday.

John announced to the dining room, "It's Harry's birthday! Champagne for everyone!" We looked at each other and thought, OK, we'll go with that, and proceeded to pour glasses of champagne for everyone in the restaurant. People were confused at first, asking, "What's the occasion?"

We replied, "It's Harry's birthday!" and they went with it. Glasses were raised as people toasted him and said:

"Thanks, Harry!"

"Happy Birthday, Harry!"

"You're the best, Harry!"

Harry just smiled and said, "You're welcome," as if he had treated everyone to champagne.

In reality, Harry didn't spend a dime, nor John. John made the announcement, we picked up the tab, and Harry got the credit. He played along perfectly. He and Mary thought it was hysterical, and we did too!

The funniest part? There was a couple on the patio celebrating their anniversary. The next year, they came back around the same time and asked, "Where's Harry? We were hoping for champagne again."

Barbecue Seafood Salad

We like the combination of shrimp, scallops, and lobster in this salad, but it is also delicious with just one or two of those. At the restaurant, we "lacquer" the seafood with barbecue sauce, which kicks up the flavor. For a simpler preparation and flavor, you can skip that step and top the salads with grilled seafood.

Spicy Mango Vinaigrette (see recipe below)

Old Bay Olive Oil Mix (see recipe on page 55)

4 large shrimp

4 large scallops

2 large cooked lobster tails, cut in half lengthwise

¼ cup **Barbecue Sauce** (see recipe on page 53) (optional)

8 ounces mixed salad greens

1 large ripe mango, peel removed, cut into slices

2 teaspoons chopped scallions

1. Make Spicy Mango Vinaigrette and set aside.

2. Grill seafood:
   Preheat oven to 400 degrees. Dip shrimp, scallops, and lobster in Old Bay Olive Oil Mix, shake off excess and grill to cook shrimp and scallops and warm the lobster. Alternatively, heat skillet over medium-high heat, dip shrimp, scallops, and lobster in Old Bay Olive Oil Mix, shake off excess, and place in hot pan, about 2-3 minutes per side to cook shrimp and scallops, and 1-2 minutes to warm the lobster.

   Transfer seafood to rimmed baking sheet, brush with Barbecue Sauce, and place in oven to finish, about 4 minutes until glazed.

3. Plate salads:
   In large bowl, toss lettuce with 3 tablespoons dressing, adding more if needed. Divide lettuce among four plates. Top each salad with scallions, mango slices, and seafood.

SERVES 4 AS ENTRÉE

Spicy Mango Vinaigrette

2 tablespoons + 2 teaspoons apple cider vinegar

¼ cup mango nectar

⅓ teaspoon chopped shallots (about a generous pinch)

¼ teaspoon each salt and pepper

¼ teaspoon crushed red pepper, or more to taste (optional)

1 teaspoon sugar

1 teaspoon honey

⅓ cup vegetable oil

In large mixing bowl, whisk together all ingredients except vegetable oil. Gradually whisk in vegetable oil until well mixed. Taste and add more salt, pepper, and vinegar if needed.

Crostini Salad

When a *Boston Globe* reviewer dined at My Place with her husband, this is what she said about the Crostini Salad: "Each bite, better than the next, confirmed we had made the right decision coming here. Our only misgiving? Next time, we'll each get our own." This salad has a following. People return year after year to enjoy it. This dish seems simple on the surface but hits all the right notes. Even the recipe tester raved about it. When a dish has that kind of loyalty, you know it's something special.

We switch up the toppings and encourage you to do the same, swapping grilled fresh tuna, shrimp, or scallops for the crab cake, or doubling up on the lobster salad. This summer lunch or light summer dinner can be prepped ahead of time and assembled at the last minute.

Crostini

1 baguette

1 tablespoon extra-virgin olive oil

Salt and Pepper Mix (see recipe on page 54)

Tuna salad

1 5-ounce can solid white albacore tuna in water, drained

¼ cup mayonnaise

8 chopped olives (Kalamata, mixed, or niçoise)

1 celery stalk, diced

Lobster salad

5 ounces freshly shucked, cooked lobster meat (tail, knuckle, and claw)

2 tablespoons mayonnaise

1 celery stalk, diced

Garden salad

4 cups lettuce

Handful halved cherry tomatoes

Handful sliced cucumber

2 thin onion slices, separated

Juice of half a lemon

Extra-virgin olive oil

Sea salt

Freshly ground pepper

Crab Cakes (see recipe on page 78)

Cocktail sauce

1. Prepare crostini:
   Cut baguette into eight ½-inch slices. Toast on grill or in 450-degree oven until golden brown, about 4 minutes. Drizzle with 1 tablespoon olive oil and sprinkle with salt and pepper.

2. Prepare lobster and tuna salads:
   In two separate bowls, toss salad ingredients lightly with mayonnaise and chopped celery. Add olives to tuna salad.

3. Plate salads:
   Toss garden salad ingredients in medium bowl and dress lightly with lemon juice, 1 tablespoon olive oil, and generous sprinkle of sea salt and pepper. Divide among four plates. Put two crostini on each plate and top with tuna and lobster salads. Finish lobster salad with flaked sea salt. Add crab cake garnished with cocktail sauce to each salad plate.

SERVES 4

Tomato Basil Corn Salad

All year long, we look forward to farm-fresh basil and just-picked sweet corn. We sprinkle corn salad over mozzarella for a craveable, peak-of-summer pizza.

5 ears corn, shucked, cooked, and cut off cob

3 ripe plum tomatoes, roughly chopped

Handful or more basil leaves, roughly chopped

1 tablespoon extra-virgin olive oil

Salt and pepper to taste

Mix all ingredients in large serving bowl. Taste and add additional salt and pepper as needed.

SERVES 4 AS A SIDE DISH

Old Bay-Seasoned Shrimp

This simple preparation elevates shrimp and gives it a delicious smoky grilled flavor.

Old Bay Olive Oil Mix (see recipe on page 55)

Salt and Pepper Mix (see recipe on page 54)

1 pound shrimp (we prefer Gulf shrimp, which are around 15 shrimp per pound, but medium-size shrimp will work well)

1. Pour Old Bay Olive Oil Mix into large bowl.

2. To grill: Dip each shrimp in Old Bay Mix, shake off excess oil, and place on hot grill grates or in grilling basket. Cook about 2 minutes, flip, and cook 2-3 minutes or until done (cooking time will depend on size of shrimp). If oil on shrimp causes a flare up, move the shrimp around to avoid creating a black film.

   To pan-sear: Heat large wok pan to medium-high heat. It's hot enough when you sprinkle a drop of water on it and it sizzles. Dip each shrimp in Old Bay Mix, shake off excess oil, and place in hot pan. Cooking in batches to avoid overcrowding the pan, sauté shrimp until nicely seared and no longer pink, about 2-3 minutes, then flip shrimp over and cook briefly (cooking time will depend on size of shrimp). If needed, add olive oil to the pan so it doesn't get too smoky.

SERVES 4-6

Sam Smith's World-Famous Barbecue Shrimp

The British singer-songwriter Sam Smith has dined here several times and was quoted in *People* magazine saying this was their favorite restaurant in the world. On Sam's first visit, they requested a shrimp dish that was gluten-free, so we created one just for them: a flavorful, smoky-sweet barbecued shrimp served with a cucumber slaw.

It was such a hit, we added it to the menu as "Sam Smith's World-Famous Barbecue Shrimp." When they returned to My Place with their mother, they saw it listed on the menu and said, "Hey, Mom, look at this—it's Sam Smith's Barbecue Shrimp."

Cucumber Slaw (see recipe on page 97)

Barbecue Sauce (see recipe on page 53)

Old Bay-Seasoned Shrimp (see recipe above)

1. Prepare Cucumber Slaw and set aside.

2. Preheat oven to 400 degrees. Prepare grilled or pan-seared Old Bay Shrimp recipe, but cook shrimp until slightly pink (it will finish cooking in the oven). Brush shrimp with Barbecue Sauce and place on rimmed baking sheet. Place in oven 3-5 minutes.

3. Divide shrimp onto four plates. Put 2-3 tablespoons water in baking pan, stir with remaining sauce, and spoon over shrimp. Serve with Cucumber Slaw for a sweet, salty, and spicy combination.

SERVES 4

Crab Cakes

These crab cakes are all about respect for the ingredient. They're packed with crab meat. Too many crab cakes get bogged down with breadcrumbs, potatoes, or a rainbow of peppers. Not these. It's a dish that embodies our cooking philosophy: Keep it simple, execute it properly, and let the food speak for itself. When preparing these, the trick is to be gentle when mixing so the crab pieces stay intact. We eat with our eyes first, so when someone orders a crab cake, they should see crab.

2 eggs

2 tablespoons Grey Poupon mustard

1 cup Hellmann's mayonnaise

2 tablespoons chopped scallions

1 tablespoon Old Bay seasoning

Pinch crushed red pepper flakes (or more to taste)

¼ teaspoon kosher salt

Pinch ground pepper

1 pound canned lump crabmeat

1 cup panko breadcrumbs

2 tablespoons unsalted butter

¼ cup extra-virgin olive oil

Cocktail sauce for serving

1. Prepare cakes:
   In large bowl, use a fork to beat the eggs. Blend in mustard, mayonnaise, scallions, Old Bay seasoning, crushed red pepper, salt, and pepper. Gently fold in crab, being careful to avoid breaking it up, then gently fold in panko. Form 12 cakes and place on a plate or tray lined with plastic. Chill for 30 minutes to firm up. You can do this step in advance and refrigerate cakes until ready to cook.

2. Sauté cakes:
   Preheat oven to 400 degrees. Have paper towel-lined plate and rimmed baking sheet ready for the cooked crab cakes. In large skillet over medium-high heat, melt butter and stir in olive oil. Heat until almost smoking. Add crab cakes in batches, being careful to avoid overcrowding them. Brown both sides, about 4 minutes per side, and then transfer to paper towel-lined plate for a few minutes, then transfer crab cakes to baking sheet.

3. Finish crab cakes in oven:
   Bake crab cakes in oven for 5-7 minutes to finish cooking. They are done when firm to the touch, with hot centers.

MAKES 12 2-OUNCE CRAB CAKES

Lobster Wontons with Spicy Cucumber Sauce

Crispy, golden, and luxuriously filled, these wontons combine lobster with Asian-inspired flavors. The tender lobster is sautéed with shallots, garlic, a hint of sherry, and our Galangal or Ginger Root Sauce before being tucked into delicate wrappers and fried until light and crunchy. Served with a tangy, spicy cucumber dipping sauce, these little bites make an elegant starter for a dinner party.

3 ounces freshly shucked, cooked lobster meat (tail, claw, and knuckle), roughly chopped

1 heaping teaspoon chopped cilantro

1 heaping teaspoon thinly sliced scallions

1 tablespoon extra-virgin olive oil

½ teaspoon chopped garlic

1 teaspoon chopped shallots

Salt and Pepper Mix (see recipe on page 54)

½ teaspoon crushed red pepper

¼ cup cream sherry

2 tablespoons **Galangal or Ginger Root Sauce** (see recipe on page 54)

¼ cup heavy cream

Wonton wrappers (we use 3 ½-inch squares)

1 egg white, beaten with 1 tablespoon water

Canola oil for frying

Sea salt

1. Make filling:
   In a small bowl, combine lobster, cilantro, and scallions and set aside.

2. Heat olive oil in large skillet or saucepan, add garlic and shallots, and sauté a few minutes until golden, being careful to avoid burning. Stir in lobster mix, pinch of salt and pepper, and crushed red pepper, and sauté 2 minutes. Add sherry, sauté 3 minutes, then add Galangal or Ginger Root Sauce and cream. Simmer at medium heat until reduced by half, about 5-7 minutes. Transfer to bowl and refrigerate at least 30 minutes. While filling is cooling, make cucumber sauce.

3. Form wontons:
   Place one wonton wrapper on a plate, brush edges with egg wash, and spoon heaping teaspoon of lobster mix into center of the wrapper. Carefully fold it over into a triangle so wrapper doesn't tear. Crimp edges with fork to seal.

4. Fry wontons:
   Have paper towel-lined plate ready. Fill deep skillet or saucepan with about 2 inches of canola oil. Heat until instant-read thermometer reads 375 degrees. Fry wontons in batches until golden brown, then transfer to plate. Sprinkle with sea salt and serve with Galangal or Ginger Root Sauce or our Quick Spicy Cucumber Sauce.

MAKES 16-18 WONTONS, DEPENDING ON SIZE OF WONTON WRAPPERS

Quick Spicy Cucumber Sauce

½ cup apple cider vinegar

½ cup simple syrup (see recipe on page 188)

2 tablespoons diced English cucumber (with peel on)

1 teaspoon crushed red pepper

½ teaspoon diced scallions

½ teaspoon chopped cilantro

Combine all ingredients in medium bowl and chill until serving.

Shrimp and Vegetable Spring Rolls

Crispy and bursting with flavor, these appetizers disappear as soon as they hit the table. A fragrant mix of shrimp, oyster mushrooms, Napa cabbage, and carrots is seasoned with our flavorful Galangal or Ginger Root Sauce, then wrapped and fried until perfectly crunchy. They're irresistible with a dipping sauce on the side. You also can skip the rolling and fry the wrappers flat for an easy, free-form version that pairs beautifully with fish.

Roughly half a head of Napa cabbage, thinly sliced (about 4 cups)

1 ½ tablespoons peanut oil

1 teaspoon chopped garlic

1 teaspoon chopped shallots

8 medium-size uncooked shrimp, shells and tails removed, diced

2 cups chopped oyster mushrooms

½ cup dry vermouth

1 cup julienned carrots

1 tablespoon oyster sauce

Galangal or Ginger Root Sauce (see recipe on page 54), divided

1 tablespoon chopped cilantro (optional)

Spring roll wrappers (not Vietnamese rice spring roll wrappers)

1 egg white beaten with 2 tablespoons water

Canola oil for frying

1. Make filling:
   Put Napa cabbage in large bowl and set aside. Heat large skillet on medium high and add peanut oil. Once oil is hot, add garlic and shallots, sautéeing for a couple minutes while stirring frequently to avoid burning. Add shrimp and sauté until shrimp is no longer pink. Stir in mushrooms and sauté for a couple minutes. Add vermouth, sauté for a couple minutes, then add carrots, oyster sauce, and ¼ cup Galangal or Ginger Root Sauce and mix until carrots are cooked but still a bit firm.

   Pour mixture over Napa cabbage and toss. Add chopped cilantro. Taste, and if needed, add another ¼ cup Galangal or Ginger Root Sauce and mix well.

2. Assemble spring rolls:
   Place spring roll wrapper onto dry surface. Lightly brush egg wash on edges. Place another wrapper on top and brush edges with egg wash.

   Spoon 3 tablespoons of filling into your hand and squeeze out excess liquid. Place filling in a horizontal line on the lower third of the wrapper. Fold left and right sides in. Roll gently away from you so you don't tear the wrapper, brush far edge with egg wash, and press to seal. Place rolls on a plate. Repeat with remaining shrimp mixture. Keep surface and your hands dry as you form the spring rolls.

3. Fry spring rolls:
   Fill deep skillet or saucepan with a couple inches of canola oil. Heat to 375 degrees (measure with instant-read or candy thermometer). Use long-handled spoon to drop spring rolls into hot oil. Fry in batches until golden brown, about 4-5 minutes, using tongs to flip spring rolls over about halfway through cooking. Transfer to paper towel-lined plate.

4. Serve spring rolls:
   Cut each roll diagonally in half and serve with Galangal or Ginger Root Sauce for dipping.

MAKES 12 ROLLS

Free-Form Spring Rolls

Serves 6

We like to serve these alongside poached salmon or halibut.

After you make the filling, fry eight spring roll wrappers flat in hot oil until crispy golden brown. The wrappers will break into pieces. Cool briefly on a paper towel-lined plate. Put about one and a half wrappers on each plate. Top with the filling and serve immediately.

Kataifi Scallops with Beurre Blanc

Scallops wrapped in kataifi are a showstopper: visually dramatic and deceptively easy to make. The key is to use fresh, local scallops. Avoid using processed scallops—they have a spongy texture and lack sweetness. When baked, the natural sugars of the scallops caramelize, the kataifi crisps up, and with a touch of scallion inside, it's a bite that surprises and delights. The beurre blanc sauce adds a delicate richness.

Kataifi is shredded filo dough available in the freezer section of many supermarkets, as well as Mediterranean and Middle Eastern specialty markets. You will want to defrost it in the refrigerator the day before making this recipe. Use the extra kataifi as a crust for seafood or vegetables, following the preparation below. Or, wrap it around fruit slices and bake for a simple-to-prep dessert.

1 package kataifi

8 scallops

2 teaspoons thinly sliced scallions

1 cup ghee or melted butter, clarified (use a spoon to skim off and discard the milk solids)

Salt and Pepper Mix (see recipe on page 54)

1. Preheat oven to 400 degrees and set to convection if possible. Pull about one third of the kataifi out of the package. On a flat surface, form four strips of kataifi, each about 2½ to 3 inches wide and about 6 inches long. Sprinkle each with ½ teaspoon chopped scallions and a pinch of salt and pepper. Place two scallops in the middle of each kataifi strip.

2. Roll the kataifi around the scallops, leaving it wispy and somewhat loose. Place on a rimmed baking sheet. Drizzle ¼ cup butter over each one.

3. Slide pan into the oven, and bake until golden brown, about 8-10 minutes, flipping halfway through. Serve each with a drizzle of beurre blanc and season with salt and pepper mix.

MAKES 4 APPETIZER SERVINGS

Beurre Blanc

4 tablespoons white wine

⅛ teaspoon minced garlic

½ teaspoon chopped shallots

Juice from 1 lemon

1 tablespoon heavy cream

1 ½ sticks butter, cut into ½-inch cubes

Salt and Pepper Mix (see recipe on page 54)

1. In medium-size skillet over medium-high heat, sauté wine, garlic, and shallots. Stir in lemon juice and cream. Once sauce is bubbling, slowly add in butter, continuing to blend with a whisk. If sauce isn't emulsifying and cream is separating from the sauce, reduce heat or briefly remove pan from heat. Season to taste.

2. Keep the sauce in a warm spot, such as on the top of the stove, but not over direct heat, so it doesn't break. You want to serve the sauce slightly warmer than room temperature.

Mussels Simmered in White Wine

I've been cooking mussels since I worked at restaurants on Nantucket, long before they became as popular as they are today. Over time, I started steaming and shucking them, serving them out of the shell to preserve their delicate flavor.

The sauce for this recipe is a white wine base with leeks, tomatoes, garlic, and herbs de Provence with a little extra tarragon, because seafood loves tarragon. We enjoy it with crostini or—better yet—our Herb Bread. I'll never forget when Len Presutti, who was the head of Martignetti Companies Wine Division, was here while we were creating the wine list. We had just been approved to sell alcohol, after being a dry town for 157 years. I paired that mussel broth with a slice of buttered Herb Bread with sea salt and a well-chilled Chablis. That synergy between the food and wine will stay with me forever; it was the perfect match.

If you want to impress your guests, make the Herb Bread in advance and serve it with good-quality butter sprinkled with sea salt and a stellar bottle of crisp French White Burgundy. Encourage your guests to dunk their bread in the broth and sip the chilled wine. I guarantee that you will have the same reaction that we had. —Kath

3 pounds mussels, rinsed in cold water, and beards removed

1 ½ cups white wine, divided

½ cup cherry tomatoes, preferably heirloom, halved

1 tablespoon chopped garlic

1 whole leek, white and light green parts cut into rings

1 ½ tablespoons herbs de Provence (if it does not contain tarragon, add a pinch of tarragon)

½ teaspoon kosher salt

½ teaspoon pepper

1 cup chicken broth

½ cup white wine

2 tablespoons unsalted butter

½ cup heavy cream

Garnish: Crostini (toasted baguette slices drizzled with extra-virgin olive oil)

1. In large pot, heat 2 cups water, mussels, and 1 cup white wine, bring to a boil then simmer, covered, for about 7 minutes until mussels open. Let cool slightly and then remove mussels from shells and place in bowl. Discard unopened or cracked mussels.

2. In large skillet, add ½ cup white wine and remaining ingredients except mussels and crostini. Simmer about 5 minutes on medium-high heat, add mussels, and simmer another 3-4 minutes. Divide into bowls and serve with crostini.

MAKES 4 DINNER OR 6 APPETIZER PORTIONS

Mussels for Eight, Please

One evening, a group of eight people came into the restaurant, and without hesitation, ordered the mussels. Every single one of them! At the end of their meal, they asked their server if Kath could stop by their table. When she did, one of the diners said, "You're not going to believe this. We were in South Africa on a tour. While we were at a film producer's house on a mountain, we were chatting with a man from Germany. We mentioned that we live in St. Louis and have a summer house in Rockport. He told us that we must go to the restaurant at the end of Bearskin Neck, and when we go, order the mussels because they are unbelievable!"

Scallops in Curry Mustard Sauce

Buttery, golden puff pastry meets tender, caramelized scallops in this elegant dish that's as impressive to serve as it is irresistible to eat. The rich, velvety sauce—made with Dijon mustard, dry vermouth, cream, and a warm hint of Madras curry—blankets the scallops and steamed vegetables in luxurious flavor. Finished with chives and juicy heirloom tomatoes, this recipe makes a stunning appetizer or entrée for a special dinner.

1 sheet frozen puff pastry, thawed in refrigerator overnight

2 tablespoons melted unsalted butter or extra-virgin olive oil

1 tablespoon extra-virgin olive oil

16 sea scallops

Salt and Pepper Mix (see recipe on page 54)

2 tablespoons chopped shallots

2 ½ tablespoons Dijon mustard

¾ cup dry vermouth

2 tablespoons Madras curry powder

2 cups heavy cream

2 cups steamed vegetables (we like thinly sliced carrots, thinly sliced zucchini, and summer squash, but many other vegetables would be delicious)

4 tablespoons chopped chives

¼ cup chopped heirloom tomatoes

Sea salt

1. Prepare puff pastry:
   Preheat oven to 450 degrees. Brush sheet pan with melted butter or olive oil. Cut four 4-inch by 4-inch squares of puff pastry, place on sheet pan, and poke pastry with a fork. Drizzle with remaining butter or oil. Bake until golden brown and crispy, about 20 minutes.

2. Cook scallops:
   Heat large skillet over medium-high heat and add 1 tablespoon olive oil. Add half of scallops to the pan and season with salt and pepper. Don't move the scallops. You want them to caramelize. Once they are nicely caramelized, flip over and cook for 1 minute. Remove scallops and place on a dish.

   If needed, add another tablespoon of oil, and once hot, add remaining scallops. Cook until caramelized, flip over and cook for 1 minute. Return first batch of scallops to pan, add shallots and Dijon mustard, shake the pan, and stir in vermouth. Turn down heat to medium. Stir in curry powder, heavy cream, and a pinch of salt and pepper and simmer for 3 minutes. Add vegetables and toss in curry sauce with the scallops.

3. Plate pastry and scallops:
   Place puff pastry squares on dishes. Top each with four scallops and vegetables. Sprinkle with chives, chopped tomatoes, and a pinch of sea salt.

SERVES 4 AS AN ENTRÉE; YOU CAN MAKE APPETIZER PORTIONS WITH 2-3 SCALLOPS EACH

A Gift from Us

She looked up and smiled. A special one grabbed her attention. It was a beauty!

As you enter, an array of hats adorn the front area. Everyone seems to enjoy the greeting from above, especially this day.

A charming couple were dining on the sun-filled deck, enjoying their time spent together. As they were ready to leave, the man stayed behind to settle. His wife wandered in front to wait for him. At that time, I said to him, "Your wife will look beautiful in this hat. It's meant for her. A gift from us. Keep it to your side when you leave, and as you walk away, slip it to her quietly." No questions asked... He was a good husband!

Several steps away, arm in arm, she turned with a smile that lit up Bearskin Neck, but not as bright as the one they gave to me! —Barb

Spicy Sizzling Shrimp

If you like a dramatic presentation for an appetizer, then you will love this! This showstopping appetizer arrives at the table still bubbling hot. Shrimp are quickly sautéed with garlic, shallots, and a splash of cream sherry, then finished with paprika, cayenne, and butter for a rich, smoky sauce. Served in a sizzling-hot bowl with plenty of bread for dipping, it's bold, aromatic, and perfect for sharing with friends over cocktails or a glass of chilled white wine.

1 tablespoon extra-virgin olive oil

10 medium uncooked shrimp, tails removed

½ teaspoon chopped garlic

1 teaspoon chopped shallots

1 cup cream sherry

2 tablespoons sweet Hungarian paprika or smoked paprika

¼ teaspoon cayenne

2 ½ to 3 tablespoons unsalted butter

Sea salt and pepper

3 tablespoons chopped scallions

Bread for dipping

1. Preheat oven to 450 degrees. Place medium-size, oven-safe bowl in the oven.

2. Heat olive oil in medium-size skillet over medium-high heat. Sauté shrimp for 1 minute, add garlic and shallots and sauté for 1 minute. Stir in sherry and sauté for 1 minute. Add paprika, cayenne, and butter, and simmer until sauce thickens and shrimp is cooked, about 1-2 minutes. Sprinkle with salt and pepper.

3. Carefully remove hot bowl from oven, place on a serving plate, and pour sizzling shrimp into hot bowl. Season with flaked sea salt and scallions. Serve family style with picks, along with bread for dipping into the sauce.

SERVES 4 AS AN APPETIZER

"Brockbuster" Prosciutto Leek Pizza

This pizza has a backstory that starts in the French Alps. We were driving through the back roads late one night when we spotted a glowing white truck in the middle of nowhere. It was a pizza truck! This was before food trucks were even a thing here. Naturally, we pulled over. The pizza was delicious, and its Gruyère cheese topping made an impression.

Back home, we started thinking about what might pair with Gruyère. We landed on crispy prosciutto and melted leeks. It was an instant hit—especially with Woody Brock, world-renowned economist and loyal regular. After repeatedly ordering the pizza, he insisted we take the pizza to New York City and name it after him. We haven't taken it to Manhattan, but we did give it his name: *The Brockbuster*.

2 tablespoons canola oil, plus more for oiling pans

4 ounces sliced prosciutto

1 tablespoon extra-virgin olive oil

¾ cup thinly sliced leeks–white and light green parts only

Pizza dough (see recipe on page 46)

1 ½ cups **My Place Tomato Sauce** (see recipe on page 57)

1 ½ cups grated cheese (we use Gruyère cheese)

2 fresh figs halved and grilled or handful of dried Mission figs (optional, but recommended!)

1. Prepare toppings:
   Line a plate with a paper towel. Heat canola oil in medium-size skillet over medium-high heat. Fry prosciutto in batches, sautéeing for 2-3 minutes per side until golden brown and very crispy. Transfer prosciutto to plate to cool.

   In medium-size skillet, warm olive oil over low-medium heat and sauté leeks until wilted and melted, but not browned, about 3-4 minutes. Remove from heat.

2. Prepare and bake pizzas:
   Preheat oven to highest possible temperature. Stretch dough and place onto pizza stone or rimless baking sheets. Spread with tomato sauce, sprinkle with cheese, and top with leeks, prosciutto, and/or figs. Bake until cheese is melted and crust is nicely browned, about 7-10 minutes.

MAKES 2 PIZZAS RANGING FROM 12 TO 16 INCHES IN DIAMETER, DEPENDING ON THICKNESS OF THE DOUGH

Chapter 3

Dance to the Music

Sandwiches and Brunch

Hump Day—
Guess What Day It Is?

Wednesday evenings in the summer, My Place hosts "Hump Day." The event is powered by DJ "Maverick," the official DJ for the Boston Red Sox, Boston Celtics, and MPBTS Hump Days. DJ Maverick, along with his wife Sheritta, and their son Jace, transform the restaurant's lower deck into a family fun dance party beneath the stars. As the sun begins to dip behind the horizon, a plane pulls a banner in capital letters stating: "GUESS WHAT DAY IT IS?!" This is My Place's way of saying, "It's summer. Let's celebrate!"

And just when it becomes dark, the fun kicks into high gear. A My Place employee or a customer leads the entire staff onto the lower deck, now a dance floor, to a chosen "walk on" song. Out they come... light-up glasses, hats, leis, and the now infamous light-up shoes. That's the signal that it's time to dance, and guests join us for line dances, singing, and even a conga line that snakes out the front door and around the end of Bearskin Neck. The neighborhood knows: It's Hump Day!

The feeling that Hump Day evokes is difficult to put into words: Happiness, celebration, and freedom, shared with family and friends in one of the most beautiful locations the world has to offer.

For many people, Wednesdays are etched forever in their memories—stunning sunsets, joyful music, and a celebration of summer; it all comes back with the words: "Guess What Day It Is?!" (And, in the mix, a camel makes an appearance)!

Crab, Shrimp, and Lobster Quiche

Rising higher than your typical quiche, this elegant, seafood-starring version is as eye-catching as it is delicious. We like the combination of crab, lobster, and shrimp for their mix of flavors and textures, but you can make it with one or two types of seafood. Baked in a buttery, tall, and flaky crust and puffed to golden perfection, it's a showstopper for brunch, lunch, or dinner. Serve it with a garden salad to round out the meal. Using a spring-form cheesecake pan emphasizes the height and flakiness of the crust.

Quiche crust

1 ½ cups all-purpose flour

10 tablespoons (1 ¼ sticks) unsalted butter

¼ teaspoon kosher salt

¼ cup ice water

Quiche filling

10 eggs

1 quart half and half

1 tablespoon kosher salt

½ teaspoon pepper

3 cups grated cheese, mix of Asiago and Gruyère

3 cups mix of cooked crab, shrimp, and lobster, chopped

1 cup chopped onion

½ cup chopped fresh tarragon or chervil (optional)

1. Make crust dough:
   In food processor, combine flour, butter, and salt. Add ice water and pulse until dough sticks together and begins to form a ball, about 1-2 minutes. Remove and knead dough until it comes together and you can form a round disc. Wrap in plastic and refrigerate for at least 30 minutes and up to 24 hours.

2. Roll out the dough:
   Place 9-inch diameter, 3-inch sided spring-form cheesecake pan on rimmed baking sheet. Spray the inside of the pan with vegetable spray.

   Use a rolling pin to roll dough into an evenly round disc that will fit into the cheesecake pan and be large enough to extend at least 2-3 inches over the pan edges. Lift dough into the pan, then press it against the bottom and up the sides, making sure there's some dough hanging over the top. Crimp top of dough over pan edge to hold crust in place and make an attractive top edge. Put pan with dough in refrigerator while you prepare filling.

3. Prepare filling:
   Preheat oven to 450 degrees. In large bowl, whisk eggs, half and half, salt, and pepper. Add cheese, seafood, onion, and herbs (if using) and mix well.

4. Assemble quiche:
   Add filling to prepared dough and slide quiche into oven. Bake 1 hour and 15 minutes, checking about halfway through. If quiche top is browning too quickly, reduce heat to 425 degrees. Bake until a knife inserted comes out clean.

5. Serve quiche:
   Trim any excess crust so it's easier to remove quiche from pan. Carefully unlock and release spring-form pan and let cool. Using two spatulas, move to large dinner plate or platter to serve. Slice and serve with garden salad.

MAKES 8-10 SERVINGS

Barbecue Salmon Sandwich with Cucumber Slaw

This sandwich strikes a perfect balance of sweet, salty, smoky, cool, and crisp. The salmon is grilled and brushed with our house-made barbecue sauce, giving it a rich, slightly sweet char. The refreshing cucumber slaw topping adds a nice crunch. For the best texture, make the slaw right before serving, and add sea salt at the last minute so it stays fresh and crunchy.

Salmon

4 salmon fillets (about 6 ounces each)

1 tablespoon Old Bay seasoning

2 tablespoons extra-virgin olive oil

½ cup **Barbecue Sauce** (see recipe on page 53)

Slaw

1 English cucumber, spiralized, or cut into long ribbons using vegetable peeler

½ teaspoon chopped garlic

2 tablespoons sour cream

2 teaspoons sea salt

4 sesame buns, split

Fresh dill or tarragon, chopped (optional)

1. Prepare salmon:
   Preheat oven to 375 degrees. Heat grill or broiler to medium-high heat. In small bowl, mix Old Bay seasoning with olive oil. Dip each salmon fillet into seasoned oil and shake off excess.

2. Mix cucumber slaw:
   While salmon is roasting, combine cucumber, garlic, sour cream, and sea salt in medium-size bowl. Taste and adjust seasonings as needed; slaw should have a salty crunch to balance the sweetness of the barbecue sauce.

3. Grill or broil salmon for about 3-4 minutes per side, until slightly charred and nearly cooked through. Place salmon on rimmed baking sheet and brush with barbecue sauce. Transfer to oven and roast 4-5 minutes, or until salmon is cooked to your liking (at least 110 degrees for medium rare) and flakes easily with a fork.

4. Assemble sandwiches:
   Lightly toast sesame buns until golden brown. Place grilled salmon fillet on the bottom half of each bun. Top with generous portion of cucumber slaw and herbs if using. Cover with top bun and serve immediately.

SERVES 4

Seafood Quesadilla

Packed with flavor, this appetizer was an instant hit with our recipe tester—so much so that the guest tasters demanded another one! Succulent lobster and shrimp tossed in Old Bay seasoning, creamy Sun-Dried Tomato Cream Cheese, and melty Monterey Jack are all tucked into a crispy, golden tortilla. It's indulgent, a little fancy, and completely irresistible. Serve it as a crowd-pleasing starter, or pair it with a crisp green salad and call it dinner.

Quesadilla

Old Bay Olive Oil Mix (see recipe on page 55)

2 ounces freshly shucked, cooked lobster meat (tail, knuckle, and claw), roughly chopped

3 medium shrimp, cooked, preferably tossed in **Old Bay Olive Oil Mix** and grilled

8-inch flour tortilla (we use Mission Carb Balance "keto wraps")

Sun-Dried Tomato Cream Cheese (see recipe on page 55)

1 tablespoon chopped scallions

2 tablespoons grated Monterey Jack cheese

Toppings

Pico de gallo

Sour cream

1. Preheat oven to 375 degrees. In medium-size bowl, combine 1 tablespoon Old Bay Olive Oil Mix, lobster, and shrimp.

2. Place flour tortilla on baking sheet and spread with thin layer of Sun-Dried Tomato Cream Cheese, roughly 3 tablespoons. Top with shrimp and lobster mixture and scallions. Sprinkle Monterey Jack cheese over quesadilla and bake face up, until golden brown and bubbling on top, about 8-15 minutes, depending on oven.

3. Fold quesadilla in half, cut into four wedges, and serve with pico de gallo and sour cream.

SERVES 4 AS APPETIZER

Warm Zucchini Salad with Grilled Shrimp

The zucchini salad originated from a recipe that Barbara used to make at home, which included sautéed zucchini, summer squash, and feta tucked into warm pita bread. This recipe takes inspiration from that sandwich, transforming it to develop a zucchini salad with shrimp and embellishments.

It's one of those sublime dishes that's packed with flavor. It's sautéed zucchini with carrots, olives, and heirloom tomatoes, tossed with pesto, topped with grilled shrimp, and finished with a little feta. People return year after year to request and enjoy it. Simple, flavorful, and perfect for a summer day on the deck.

Old Bay-Seasoned Shrimp (see recipe on page 77)

2 tablespoons extra-virgin olive oil, plus more for dressing and drizzling

2 tablespoons chopped shallots

1 tablespoon thinly sliced leeks

4 cups thinly sliced zucchini (from 2 medium or 3 small zucchini)

4 cups thinly sliced summer squash (from 2 medium squash)

¼ cup chicken broth
1 cup halved cherry tomatoes, preferably heirloom

½ cup pitted Kalamata olives

4 tablespoons **Pesto** (see recipe on page 57)

½ cup crumbled feta cheese, plus more for sprinkling

Small handful julienned carrots

8 cups green leaf or other lettuce of your choice

¼ cup thinly sliced sweet onion

Salt and Pepper Mix (see recipe on page 54)

1 lemon

1. Cook shrimp:
   Prepare grilled or pan-seared Old Bay-Seasoned Shrimp and set aside.

2. Prepare vegetables:
   Heat olive oil in wok-style pan or large skillet on medium heat. Add shallots and leeks and sauté until soft, stirring frequently to avoid browning, about 2-3 minutes. Add zucchini, summer squash, and chicken broth, sauté for about 3 minutes. Stir in tomatoes and olives and sauté until zucchini and summer squash are al dente and have a sauce-like consistency. Season with salt and pepper. Mix in pesto, feta cheese, and carrots and remove from heat.

3. Plate salads:
   In large bowl, toss lettuce and onion with squeeze of lemon juice, 2 tablespoons olive oil, and pinch of salt and pepper. Divide salad among four plates and top with zucchini mixture, shrimp, and sprinkle of feta.

SERVES 4

Inspiration for the Decibel Sour

The early days of our Hump Day tradition (see page 94 for Hump Day– Guess What Day It Is) were quite tumultuous, but for reasons we never anticipated.

If you aren't a local, you might not know that Rockport is fundamentally a sleepy little town with very little nightlife. We figured Hump Day would provide a bit of liveliness for all ages, particularly our frequent patrons ranging from ages 4 to 95. It's just plain fun to dance the Macarena with friends and neighbors of all ages on a warm, moonlit night. Our summertime Wednesday evening festivities—featuring music and dancing on our outdoor deck overlooking the ocean—were loved by all, with one exception.

After our first Hump Day, a neighbor complained that our guests' joyous dancing, singing, and laughing disrupted their business. We tried to win them over with friendly conversations and offers of hospitality, pointing out that Hump Day festivities boosted Bearskin Neck foot traffic and offered visitors a novel experience previously unavailable in Rockport. Plus, Hump Day is only once a week from 5 p.m. to 10 p.m. in the summertime, weather permitting. So, at the most, there would be about 12 evenings of joy per year, advertised on the same night by a Piper Cub small plane pulling a banner asking, "Guess What Day It Is?" But it was to no avail.

Despite the many positive aspects of the event, our adversary took many actions to discourage us. Specifically, the neighbor installed a decibel counter on their property, took numerous photos documenting the event, and mailed complaint letters to the town's Board of Selectmen. They even brought the matter of Hump Day and the lively music to a Town Meeting, asking the residents to vote on whether My Place needed to adhere to a specific decibel count limit. (For background, decibels are the units used to measure sound intensity.) At that meeting, 97% of Rockport voters sided with us. Not a single person spoke out against Hump Day. In fact, many people asked for event details so they could join in the fun!

We returned to the restaurant that night feeling victorious. To our delight, a group of African healers accompanying a group of HIV/AIDS research scientists were dining with us. They had just landed a major grant and celebrated by breaking into spontaneous drumming, singing, and dancing on the restaurant's second floor. We joined them in celebration and energetic dancing. You can find a video of this on our Facebook page.

Over the years, Hump Day inspired quite a few t-shirt designs. One of our favorites reads: "Only in Rockport can you have this much fun and be in bed by 10:30." (Credit for that brilliant line goes to tax assessor Chris Trupiano.) To commemorate our Town Meeting victory, we also introduced a new cocktail, The Decibel Sour. One of our art-student servers even designed a shirt to celebrate it.

Decibel Sour

2 scoops lemon sorbet

2 ounces vodka

2 ounces limoncello

2 ounces peach schnapps

2 ounces lemonade

2 ounces sour mix

Fresh squeeze of lemon

2-3 cups of ice

Garnish: 2 lemon wedges

Add all ingredients except garnish to blender and mix well. Serve in coupe or martini glasses garnished with lemon wedges.

MAKES 2 DRINKS

Chicken and Brie Sandwich

Many regulars love this sandwich so much that they've never tried anything else on the menu. Its appeal may be the subtle tang of the just-melting brie, combined with juicy grilled chicken, the hint of onion flavor from the scallions, and the heirloom tomato topping—all nestled in a good-quality, crusty baguette.

8 ounces grilled chicken breast, cut into ⅛-inch to ¼-inch-thick slices

10-inch baguette, cut in half width wise and lengthwise

1 tablespoon chopped scallions

4 ounces brie cheese, cut into ⅛-inch-thick slices

2 tablespoons diced heirloom cherry tomatoes

Sea salt and pepper

1. Preheat oven to 450 degrees. Place chicken slices in two piles on small, rimmed sheet pan. Sprinkle chopped scallions on top of chicken. Top with brie slices, covering chicken as much as possible so it does not dry out. Heat in oven until the cheese melts, about 3-4 minutes.

2. While chicken and cheese are heating, place baguette pieces on plates. Remove chicken and cheese and place on baguette with brie on top. Sprinkle each sandwich with diced tomatoes and season with salt and pepper.

SERVES 2

Will Hart worked in the kitchen and his sister Alex was a server. Will eventually became a minister assigned to work in a remote village in Africa, helping the community build infrastructure. While there, he lived in a tent with no electricity or running water. Alex went to visit. One night in the tent they were reminiscing about summer days at My Place by the Sea when they began talking about the Chicken and Brie Sandwich, with its grilled chicken with just-melting cheese, tomatoes, and scallions on the crispy baguette. They had to stop talking about it because their mouths were watering! First stop home... My Place with the story and a Chicken and Brie, please!!

Variation: Instead of the brie, brush each sandwich with 1 tablespoon Chipotle Mayonnaise (see page 54), and add lettuce and two slices cooked applewood smoked bacon.

Roasted Vegetable and Artichoke Sandwich

This sandwich showcases some of our favorite Mediterranean flavors—sweet red, orange, and yellow roasted peppers; earthy mushrooms; tender artichokes; a vibrant, emerald pesto; and a generous sprinkle of quality feta cheese. Be sure to use fresh-baked ciabatta rolls or a high-quality French baguette; the crusty bread soaks up the juices and offers a texture that contrasts nicely with the vegetable filling.

It's a simple sandwich, while at the same time incredibly flavorful and attractive to the eye. Many have said that the sandwich is the best vegetarian sandwich they've ever had!

1 tablespoon extra-virgin olive oil

4 cups thinly sliced red, orange, and yellow bell peppers (from 3 medium-size peppers)

Salt and Pepper Mix (see recipe on page 54)

1 cup large white mushrooms

6 canned artichoke hearts, drained and sliced

Heaping ¼ cup **Pesto** (see recipe on page 57)

4 tablespoons crumbled feta cheese (optional)

4 fresh-baked ciabatta rolls or good-quality French baguette cut into 4 6-inch segments

1. Cook vegetables:
   Preheat oven to 450 degrees. Heat olive oil in medium-size skillet over medium-high heat. Add peppers and sauté, stirring, for 3-4 minutes until slightly softened, and sprinkle with pinch of salt and pepper. Transfer peppers to bowl. Grill mushrooms until they have grill marks, which gives them a smoky flavor, then cut into slices when cool enough to handle. Alternatively, cut mushrooms into thick slices, add to skillet, and sauté until softened, then sprinkle with pinch of salt and pepper.

2. Finish in oven:
   On a rimmed baking sheet, toss peppers, mushrooms, and artichoke slices with pesto. Sprinkle with feta and pinch of salt and pepper, and heat in oven, tossing after 3 minutes, and bake until golden brown, about 5-7 minutes total.

3. Assemble sandwiches:
   Place bread on four plates and fill with vegetable and feta mixture.

SERVES 4

Summer Pesto Pasta Salad

This salad is perfect for picnics, dinners on the deck, and lunch at the beach.

2 cups orecchiette or penne pasta (we only use De Cecco brand)

1 ½ cups or more **Tomato Basil Corn Salad** (see recipe on page 76)

1 tablespoon extra-virgin olive oil

4 tablespoons **Pesto** (see recipe on page 57)

Sea salt

1 tablespoon or more grated Asiago, Pecorino, Parmesan, or other dry grating cheese

Cook pasta according to package instructions and drain. In large serving bowl, combine pasta, Tomato Basil Corn Salad, olive oil, and Pesto. Top with sprinkle of sea salt and cheese.

SERVES 4-6 AS APPETIZER

Tuna and Farm Fresh Egg Salad

Chunky albacore tuna, creamy avocado, and heirloom cherry tomatoes mingle with tender greens, briny Kalamata olives, and perfectly cooked eggs in this popular salad. It's all about simplicity and high-quality ingredients. A drizzle of fruity olive oil, a squeeze of lemon, and a pinch of sea salt tie it all together. It's ideal for an effortless lunch, a light dinner, or a no-fuss picnic.

4 eggs

2 5-ounce cans solid white albacore tuna, drained and left in chunks

12 pitted Kalamata olives

1 ½ cups halved heirloom cherry tomatoes

2 avocados, sliced

8-10 ounces fresh lettuce greens, local if possible

1 lemon

Garnish: High-quality, fruity olive oil

Sea salt

1. Prepare eggs:
   Fill medium-size bowl with ice and cold water and set aside. Fill medium saucepan ¾ full with water and bring to boil. Using a long-handled spoon, place eggs in water and boil for 9 minutes. Transfer eggs to ice bath. Once cool, peel eggs and refrigerate. This step can be done a day in advance.

2. Plate salads:
   Divide lettuce among four plates. Place tuna around lettuce, sprinkle with olives, tomatoes, and avocado slices. Cut each egg in half lengthwise and add to salads. Garnish with a squeeze of fresh lemon, good fruity extra-virgin olive oil, and a sprinkle of sea salt.

SERVES 4

Vegetable Skewers with Lebanese-Style Rice

Golden roasted vegetables with a crispy Dijon and panko crust pair beautifully with fragrant Lebanese-style rice tossed with pine nuts, parsley, currants, and a touch of pasta. We created this for our vegan friends who were seeking satiating, flavorful comfort food.

1 medium zucchini, cut in 1-inch rounds

1 medium summer squash, cut in 1-inch rounds

1 large red pepper, seeds and ribs removed, cut in 2-inch squares

1 large orange pepper, seeds and ribs removed, cut in 2-inch squares

8 medium-size, canned artichoke hearts, drained

4 large white mushrooms, stems removed, cut in half

½ cup Dijon mustard

1 ¼ cups panko breadcrumbs

2 tablespoons extra-virgin olive oil, plus more for drizzling

1 cup cubed butternut squash, roasted or steamed, or 1 cup **Tomato Basil Corn Salad** (see recipe on page 76) (optional)

¼ cup diced heirloom tomatoes or other good-tasting tomato

Sea salt and pepper

1. **Prepare skewers:**
   Preheat oven to 425 degrees. If using wooden skewers, soak in water for 20 minutes. Thread vegetables onto four skewers, alternating between vegetables. Brush with Dijon mustard and roll in panko breadcrumbs. If serving with Lebanese-Style Rice, follow steps 1-3 in rice recipe.

2. **Bake skewers:**
   Pour oil onto rimmed baking sheet and place in oven for 5 minutes to warm the oil. Remove pan, place skewers in pan, and return to oven for 10 minutes. Flip skewers and roast until vegetables are easily pierced with a knife, about 10 minutes.

3. **Plate vegetables:**
   Place skewers on plates, with golden brown side facing up. Carefully remove skewers. Drizzle each with a teaspoon olive oil, then sprinkle with butternut squash or Tomato Basil Corn Salad (if using), diced tomatoes, sea salt, and pepper. Serve with Lebanese-Style Rice.

SERVES 4

Lebanese-Style Rice

1 cup uncooked rice

1 teaspoon plus 1 tablespoon extra-virgin olive oil

2 tablespoons pine nuts or other nut of choice

1 tablespoon chopped parsley

½ cup cooked, chopped pasta (we only use De Cecco brand angel hair)

2 tablespoons currants or raisins

Sea salt

Pepper

1. Preheat oven to 350 degrees. Put rice, 1 ½ cups water, and 1 teaspoon olive oil in small saucepan over high heat. Bring to a boil, cover and reduce heat, and simmer 15 minutes or until liquid is absorbed.

2. Remove from heat and let sit, covered, for 10 minutes. Fluff with a fork.

3. While rice is cooking, place nuts on baking sheet and toast until golden brown, about 4-5 minutes. Transfer to plate to cool.

4. In large serving bowl, combine cooked rice with nuts, parsley, pasta, currants, and 1 tablespoon olive oil. Season with sea salt and pepper.

SERVES 4

Please God Heal Her Now by Judi Rotenberg

Chapter 4

Ain't No Mountain High Enough

Entrées

The Soldier's Dinner

Years ago, we received a phone call late at night. The caller ID showed a number ending in triple zeroes—a clear sign it was coming from far away. When we picked up, we were stunned to learn just how far. The call was from Afghanistan from a sergeant in the U.S. Army.

He told us that his wife had seen a *Chronicle* television segment about our restaurant and had always dreamed of dining with us. Her birthday was coming up, and he wanted to make it unforgettable.

"I know you have a same-day reservation policy," he said, "but is there any chance you could make an exception?"

Without hesitation, we said, "Absolutely! And, can we bake her a cake?"

When the special evening arrived, his wife came with a friend and we seated them at a patio table overlooking the water. We took care of everything. At the end of the meal, we presented her with a birthday cake, decorated with the words "I love you," followed by the soldier's name, John.

She immediately burst into tears. Her friend began crying. Soon, surrounding guests on the patio were in tears, too. Our servers got emotional and so did we. These were happy tears because of the soldier's loving gesture, but also tears of concern for a couple separated by many thousands of miles, and facing the uncertainties that come with military service.

That same night, just after midnight, we received another call from the triple-zero number. It was the soldier again—this time, his voice was breaking.

"Thank you so much for making her birthday so special," he said. "I'm going to fly a flag in your honor for 30 days here in Afghanistan." And so he did.

We invited him to visit us when he returned home. Months later, he and his wife came for a romantic dinner on the deck on a warm summer evening. We treated them to dinner and champagne.

Before leaving, he told us he would fly another flag for us when he redeployed—and once again, he kept his promise, this time flying a flag in Iraq in our honor.

Eventually, both American flags arrived by mail, each accompanied by an official letter of authenticity.

That July 4th, after we received the first flag, we held a small ceremony and unfurled the flag from our top deck. Mark Silva, owner of The Strudel Shop and a career serviceman, attended in his army uniform. With heartfelt reverence, he stood beneath the flag and saluted.

Szechuan Salmon with Asian Noodle Pancakes

This recipe goes back to Kathy's time as chef at the Peabody Essex Museum. When the museum's director of public relations tasted the Szechuan Salmon and said she was from the Sichuan region of China—and loved the dish—it felt like a true compliment. We like to serve Szechuan Salmon with Asian Noodle Pancakes (see accompanying recipe). But if you are short on time, serve it with steamed rice or cooked noodles. Because this recipe comes together quickly, you will want to have all ingredients chopped before you begin cooking the salmon.

Salmon

1 ½-pounds skinless salmon fillet, cut into 4 pieces

1 tablespoon sesame oil

1 tablespoon peanut oil (don't substitute with another oil)

Szechuan sauce

1 tablespoon peanut oil (don't substitute with another oil)

1 tablespoon sesame oil

1 teaspoon minced garlic

1 teaspoon minced shallots

1 cup sliced oyster or other type mushroom

1 leek, white and green parts thoroughly washed and thinly sliced into rings

1 cup thinly sliced bell peppers, snow peas, or mix of both

1 pinch to 1 teaspoon crushed red pepper

¼ cup dry vermouth

1 cup chicken broth

1 cup hoisin sauce

Garnish: Cilantro or parsley sprigs

Salt and Pepper Mix (see recipe on page 54)

Asian Noodle Pancakes (see recipe on page 114), steamed rice, or noodles

1. If you are serving this with Asian Noodle Pancakes, prepare them first.

2. Prepare salmon:
Preheat oven to 375 degrees. Have rimmed baking sheet ready. Pat salmon dry with paper towel and check for bones, removing any you find. Sprinkle salmon with salt and pepper and put on plate. Heat large skillet with sesame oil and peanut oil until smoking hot. Sear salmon until crispy and golden brown, about 3-4 minutes. Flip over and remove skillet from heat.

   Transfer salmon to baking sheet and slide into oven to finish cooking. Check after 4 minutes. Roast until a thermometer in the thickest part of the fish reaches 110-130 degrees, depending on your preference for doneness.

3. Make Szechuan sauce:
In same large skillet, heat 1 tablespoon peanut oil and 1 tablespoon sesame oil and sauté garlic and shallots for 30 seconds. Add mushrooms, leeks, bell peppers, and crushed red pepper, stirring and being careful to avoid browning the garlic. When mushrooms begin to soften, add vermouth and sauté about 2 minutes to cook off alcohol.

Haddock

You can also make Szechuan Haddock, which is best served with jasmine rice.

Prepare Baked Gloucester Haddock (see recipe on page 128), and prepare Szechuan sauce, starting with step 3 at left.

Stir in chicken broth and hoisin sauce and simmer 3-4 minutes to thicken. If it's too thick, add a couple extra spoonfuls of broth or water. Taste sauce and add more crushed red pepper if it needs more heat, more hoisin sauce for sweetness, and salt if needed. Return salmon to pan with Szechuan sauce briefly to warm it.

4. Plate the salmon:
Place a pancake or cooked rice or noodles on each plate and ladle a couple of spoonfuls of sauce over it. Top with salmon and drizzle the remaining sauce over each salmon fillet. Garnish with cilantro or parsley and serve immediately.

SERVES 4

Asian Noodle Pancakes

Have you ever tasted something that was so memorable that it stayed with you for years? Someone who waited tables here for just one season—about 25 years ago—called Kathy out of the blue from Virginia. He was opening a waterfront spot and couldn't stop thinking about our Asian Noodle Pancake that he had tasted while he was here. He asked Kath to give him the recipe and if it would be OK to serve at his restaurant.

½ pound good-quality angel hair pasta, thin spaghetti, or linguine (we only serve De Cecco brand pasta for all our pasta dishes)

Peanut oil for frying

Sesame oil for frying

2 tablespoons chopped shallots, divided

4 tablespoons chopped scallions, divided

Salt and Pepper Mix (see recipe on page 54)

1. Cook pasta:
   Cook pasta according to package instructions, but do not add oil to cooking water. Drain pasta in colander.

2. Form pancakes:
   Line a baking sheet with paper towels. Heat small skillet (ideally an 8-inch pan) to medium-high and add 1 ½ tablespoons of peanut oil and 1 tablespoon sesame oil.

3. Once the oil is hot and nearly smoking, add about one-quarter of the cooked pasta (roughly 1 heaping cup) in a clump to the pan. Sprinkle with one-quarter of the shallots and scallions and season with salt and pepper. Leave undisturbed to crisp and become golden brown on outer edges, about 4 minutes. Use a spatula to turn pancake over, then cook until golden brown on the other side.

4. Transfer pancake to paper towel-lined baking sheet. Repeat to make the remaining pancakes, adding more peanut oil to the pan as needed, 1 tablespoon at a time. Serve pancakes at room temperature or briefly warm in the oven after removing paper towels from baking sheet.

MAKES 4 PANCAKES

When was it that My Place became Our Place?

We were already frequent visitors to Barb and Kathy's wonderful restaurant, but something changed one beautiful summer day in 2016.

Over Kathy's special lunch and a bottle of Paul Hobbs Chardonnay, we made the decision to change our lives together. This was when My Place became a central part of our lives.

Here's the backstory: The two of us were reunited in 2009 after many years apart. Then in 2015, Viv moved from Louisville to Annisquam, where we rented a cottage together. Soon after, we decided to search for a house that we might buy together on Cape Ann. After several months, we saw a special house on Marmion Way in Rockport that our dear friends, Ken and Marianne Novack, were selling. We were enchanted, and after a second visit on that 2016 summer day, we had lunch at My Place to discuss the life-changing step of buying a home together.

Soon after, we bought the house and then built our current home. When it was completed, we planned our move, with our first night there to be on August 17, 2018. We knew that dinner on August 17th would of course be—where else?—at My Place by the Sea. What Vivienne did not know was that Michael planned to propose to her right before dinner.

Of course, Barb and Kathy already knew everything! When we walked in for the dinner that Friday evening, newly engaged, everyone else in the restaurant already knew and began applauding! We were seated at a favorite patio table, which was adorned with beautiful flowers from Ken and Marianne. Kathy and Barb treated us to dinner.

From then on, special My Place moments and memories continued. Kathy and Barb became family, and every dinner with them became a homecoming! Though we love many of Kathy's dishes, we developed favorites over these months: her wonderful Tempura Shrimp, her Raspberry Orange Salad, and her amazing Szechuan Haddock with jasmine rice.

On December 30, 2019, our families gathered upstairs at My Place for a pre-wedding ceremony dinner. We returned home after this wonderful dinner and were married the same evening, just after midnight, on New Years Eve, 2019.

When the pandemic hit us all in March 2020, two short months after our wedding, Kathy and Barb fed us regularly with special takeout dinners, usually featuring Szechuan Haddock, the ultimate comfort food; Vivienne credits that dish for saving her sanity and sustaining our new marriage throughout the nearly two years of lockdown.

Our first dinner out after vaccines arrived and before most places had reopened took place at My Place early the following year, outside, with Ken and Marianne, with each couple seated 10 feet apart, at nearby tables on the upstairs porch.

There have been so many special times since at Our Place: dinners with family, with friends, Hump Day nights ("We heard there would be dancing"), quiet celebrations of special occasions, memorable evenings with visiting family and friends, the last restaurant dinner out that we ever had with Mike's father, Teddy and Patrick's wedding celebration, quiet lunches with each other and with Ken, always magical.

What is it that makes My Place by the Sea so magical? It begins with our dear friends Kathy and Barb, who are so generous, kind, and thoughtful. It continues with the gorgeous setting of this special restaurant on the ocean at the end of Bearskin Neck. We are still enchanted each time we enter, greeted by Barb and her staff, and throughout each wonderful meal from Kathy, as it unfolds. There is magic in the warmth and love that we feel on every visit, which culminates each time with Kathy's tableside visit as the meal service is winding down, and we all have a chance to catch up. And did we mention the Szechuan Haddock?

—Vivienne and Michael Mendelsohn

Swordfish with Béarnaise Sauce and Pecan Butter

Tender swordfish meets nutty pecan butter and a velvety béarnaise sauce. The tarragon gives it a distinct flavor that complements the richness of the sauce. Don't be intimidated by the béarnaise sauce—this version is foolproof if all the ingredients are the same temperature.

Serve with steamed red bliss potatoes drizzled with butter and sea salt and seasonal vegetables.

Tarragon reduction

½ cup red wine vinegar

1 tablespoon dried tarragon

½ tablespoon chopped shallots

Pecan butter

3 tablespoons unsalted butter

½ cup chopped pecans

Swordfish

½ cup panko or plain breadcrumbs

2 teaspoons paprika

4 6-ounce swordfish fillets

¼ cup mayonnaise

6 tablespoons ghee or clarified butter

Salt and Pepper Mix (see recipe on page 54)

Béarnaise sauce

5 ounces (10 tablespoons) ghee or clarified butter

1 egg and 1 egg yolk

Tiny pinch cayenne pepper

Juice of 1 lemon

1. Make tarragon reduction:
   In a small saucepan over medium heat, combine red wine vinegar, tarragon, and shallots. Simmer until most of the liquid has evaporated, about 3 minutes. Set aside to cool.

2. Prepare pecan butter:
   Melt butter in small pan over medium heat. Add pecans, season with salt and pepper, and sauté for 2-3 minutes until fragrant. Remove from heat.

3. Roast swordfish:
   Preheat oven to 450 degrees. In large bowl, mix panko or plain breadcrumbs and season with salt and pepper, and paprika. Brush swordfish fillet tops with mayonnaise and coat with seasoned breadcrumbs. Drizzle with ghee or clarified butter. Place on rimmed baking sheet and add 4 tablespoons warm water to the bottom of the pan. Bake until fish is tender when pierced with a knife or when a thermometer in the thickest part of the fish reaches 110-130 degrees, depending on your preference for doneness, about 10-12 minutes.

4. Prepare béarnaise sauce while swordfish is roasting:
The key to successfully making this sauce is ensuring all ingredients are warm when blended. Place lemon and eggs in a small bowl, cover with 2 cups hot water, and set aside to temper. Squeeze juice from warmed lemon and set aside. Heat ghee or clarified butter to be hot to the touch.

To clarify butter: Heat butter in microwave or small saucepan over medium heat until melted. Use a spoon to skim off and discard the white milk solids that float to the top.

In food processor, add egg and egg yolk and process. While machine is running, slowly add ghee or clarified butter so it emulsifies and reaches a pudding-like consistency. While processor is running, add lemon juice, tarragon reduction, salt, and pepper. Taste and add more lemon juice if needed to achieve a lemony flavor.

5. Plate swordfish:
If needed, gently rewarm the pecan butter. Place swordfish on plates. Spoon pecan butter over fillets, drizzle with béarnaise sauce, and serve immediately.

SERVES 4

Coconut Curried Noodles

Noodles are tossed in a velvety coconut curry sauce that is equal parts creamy, savory, and just the right amount of spice. A rainbow of vegetables keeps it bright and fresh, while roasted peanuts add crunch. Customize it to your taste, adding more or less curry paste and your choice of tofu, shrimp, or chicken. Our recipe tester and her family liked this so much that they've enjoyed it multiple times.

12 ounces lo mein noodles, rice noodles, or fettuccine

2 tablespoons peanut or vegetable oil

1 tablespoon finely chopped shallots

1 ½ teaspoons minced garlic

1 cup thinly sliced leeks

1 ½ to 2 tablespoons red curry paste (depending on your spice preference)

¼ cup dry white vermouth or vegetable broth

1 cup chopped vegetables (we like a mixture of bell peppers, snap peas, and carrots)

Protein of your choice:
- 12 ounces to 1 pound peeled and deveined shrimp
- Thinly sliced, grilled chicken breast or
- 1 cup cubed tofu (see tofu method below)

1 14-ounce can coconut milk

2 tablespoons hoisin sauce

2 tablespoons brown sugar

Salt and Pepper Mix (see recipe on page 54)

¼ cup chopped roasted peanuts

¼ cup chopped fresh cilantro

Tofu cooking method

1 package extra-firm tofu

1 tablespoon extra-virgin olive oil

Salt and Pepper Mix (see recipe on page 54)

1. Preheat oven to 425 degrees. Remove tofu from package, rinse under cold water, and pat dry with a clean kitchen towel or paper towel to remove as much liquid as possible. Cut into ¾-inch cubes.

2. Place tofu cubes on rimmed baking sheet. Toss with olive oil to coat and sprinkle generously with salt and pepper. Roast in the oven until crispy, about 20 minutes, flipping cubes with spatula about halfway through baking.

---

1. Prepare noodles:
Cook noodles according to package instructions. Drain, rinse in cold water, and set aside.

2. Make curry sauce:
Heat oil in large pan or wok over medium heat. Add shallots and garlic and sauté until fragrant, about 1-2 minutes. Stir in leeks and cook for another 2 minutes, ensuring they soften but do not brown.

Stir in curry paste and cook for 1 minute. Carefully pour in vermouth and simmer until alcohol burns off, 2-3 minutes. Add vegetables and protein of choice. If adding shrimp, stir-fry until shrimp is cooked. Stir in coconut milk, hoisin sauce, and sugar. Season with salt and pepper and simmer for 5 minutes. Add noodles to the pan, tossing to coat evenly in the sauce, 1-2 minutes until noodles are hot.

3. Plate curried noodles:
Divide noodle mixture onto four plates. Sprinkle with chopped roasted peanuts and fresh cilantro.

SERVES 4

Cedar Plank-Roasted Salmon with Vegetables

We like roasting salmon on a cedar plank because it imparts a subtle flavor without being smoky, plus it makes the salmon a bit crunchy on the outside while staying silky on the inside. This method doesn't need any oil added to the fish, making it lower in fat. We suggest serving it with steamed jasmine rice and a ragú of seasonal vegetables.

½ pound haricot verts (thin green beans) or green beans, trimmed

4 5-ounce salmon fillets

2 tablespoons extra-virgin olive oil

1-2 tablespoons chopped shallots

1 medium zucchini, thinly sliced

1 medium summer squash, thinly sliced

½ cup cherry tomatoes, cut in half

½ cup thinly sliced scallions

8 Kalamata olives

1 cup chicken or vegetable broth

Sea salt

Freshly ground pepper

Steamed jasmine rice and cooked carrots for serving

1. Presoak cedar plank in water for at least 30 minutes and up to 24 hours in advance. Don't skip this step—the plank is flammable unless soaked.

You can find treated cedar planks at a lumber yard and have them cut. We use 12-inch by 7-inch planks. The planks also are sold by many seafood purveyors.

---

2. Blanch haricot verts:
Add ice and cold water to a large bowl and set aside. Bring a large pot of water to boil, add haricot verts, and boil for about 2-3 minutes until they are bright green and slightly tender but still have a snap. Use a slotted spoon to transfer them to the bowl of ice water. Finish this step before proceeding with the recipe (this step can be done hours or a day in advance).

3. Roast salmon:
Preheat oven to 450 degrees. Place a rimmed baking sheet or sheet of aluminum foil on the lower oven rack to catch any runoff from the plank. Remove cedar plank from soaking water. Place salmon on plank and season with freshly ground pepper and sea salt, which will help produce an outer crust. Slide the plank directly into oven and roast 10-15 minutes until a thermometer in the thickest part of the fish reaches 110-130 degrees, depending on your preference for doneness. While salmon is roasting, prepare vegetables.

4. Make vegetable ragú:
Heat olive oil over medium-high in hot wok-style pan. Stir in shallots and sauté for 1 minute. Add zucchini, summer squash, haricot verts, cherry tomatoes, scallions, and olives and sauté until vegetables are al dente. Add broth and simmer about 3-4 minutes to make sauce, which will be brothy with a sunset color. Sprinkle with sea salt.

5. Serve salmon:
Place rice in bowls. Spoon vegetables and some broth over rice, top with salmon, and drizzle remaining broth over salmon.

SERVES 4

Pesto Prosciutto-Wrapped Halibut with Roasted Summer Vegetables

Savory prosciutto, fragrant basil pesto, and tender local halibut join forces in this impressive and flavorful dish. The salty prosciutto crisps beautifully in the pan, locking in the halibut's moisture while the pesto infuses each bite with brightness. Paired with a generous side of roasted summer vegetables and finished with a dollop of Basil Aioli, it's a colorful, Mediterranean-inspired dish that's perfect for a dinner party as well as a weeknight dinner.

Basil Aioli

1 heaping tablespoon **Pesto**

1 cup mayonnaise

Combine until well mixed.

6 ounces Prosciutto di Parma (12 slices)

6 tablespoons **Pesto** (see recipe on page 57)

6 6-ounce halibut pieces

Salt and Pepper Mix (see recipe on page 54)

Extra-virgin olive oil

Basil Aioli (see recipe at left)

1. If serving with Roasted Summer Vegetables, begin cooking vegetables 45 minutes before you prepare the halibut. Prepare Basil Aioli.

2. Prepare halibut:
   Preheat oven to 450 degrees. Lay two prosciutto pieces horizontally on cutting board or other flat surface. Holding piece of halibut skin side down, brush top with 1 tablespoon pesto and place face down, vertically. Season with salt and pepper and wrap prosciutto around halibut with prosciutto seam on the bottom, skin side of the fish.

3. Cook halibut:
   Heat about 1 tablespoon olive oil in large oven-safe skillet over medium heat. Once oil is hot, place halibut pesto side up. Sear until nicely browned, about 5 minutes. Flip fish over and place skillet in oven to finish cooking, about 5 minutes or until a thermometer in the thickest part of the fish reaches 110-130 degrees.

4. Serve with Roasted Summer Vegetables (see recipe on facing page) and garnish of Basil Aioli.

SERVES 6

Roasted Summer Vegetables

1 Spanish onion or three shallots, quartered

3 medium zucchini, cut into 1-inch slices

3 summer squash, cut into 1-inch slices

6 plum tomatoes, tops cut off, cut in half lengthwise

2 small to medium fennel bulbs, trimmed, core removed, cut into ½-inch slices

¼ cup loosely packed, fresh basil leaves

¼ cup pitted French olives or Kalamata olives

¼ cup extra-virgin olive oil

3 cups **My Place Tomato Sauce** (see recipe on page 57)

1 cup chicken or vegetable broth

1 teaspoon **Salt and Pepper Mix** (see recipe on page 54)

Preheat oven to 450 degrees. Mix all ingredients in large roasting pan, cover with aluminum foil, and roast for 1 hour or until soft.

SERVES 6-8 AS A SIDE DISH

Local Haddock with Lemon, Garlic, and White Wine Sauce

You have Roger Dagorn, master sommelier and wine director of The River Café in Brooklyn, to thank for this recipe's place in this book. While dining at My Place during our final days of recipe testing, he tasted this dish and asked, "Of course the haddock recipe will be in the book?" We replied, "Of course!"—then promptly wrote it down and sent it to Amy to edit and test.

This dish captures the My Place ethos: simple, beautifully prepared food made with high-quality ingredients. The lemony sauce is rich and flavorful, especially when paired with potato purée, rice, or fresh organic vegetables. For a lighter version, dial back the cream and add a bit more broth.

1 tablespoon (enough to coat bottom of pan) extra-virgin olive oil

1 ½ teaspoons chopped garlic

1 cup sliced large mushrooms

Juice from 1 lemon

1 cup white wine

½ cup chicken or fish stock

2 tablespoons unsalted butter

8 pitted olives of your choice (we prefer niçoise, and Kalamata olives are also good)

½ cup halved heirloom cherry tomatoes

1 cup heavy cream

Baked Gloucester Haddock (see recipe on page 128 and make this sauce instead of the Salsa de Juel; omit panko coating for a gluten-free version)

Salt and Pepper Mix (see recipe on page 54)

Garnish: Fresh parsley, tarragon, or chervil, or combination

1. Prepare haddock according to recipe on page 128.

2. While haddock is baking, prepare sauce:
   In large skillet, heat olive oil over medium heat and sauté garlic until lightly browned and aromatic, being careful to avoid burning it. Stir in mushrooms and sauté until they begin to turn golden brown in color. Add lemon juice, wine, and chicken stock and simmer 3-4 minutes.

   Add butter, olives, tomatoes, and heavy cream. Cook on medium-high to bring to a boil, then turn down heat to simmer until sauce reduces to desired consistency. Taste and season with salt and pepper.

3. Plate haddock:
   If serving with vegetables and potatoes or rice, divide those onto plates. Place haddock fillets on plates, spoon sauce on top, and garnish with fresh herbs of your choice.

SERVES 4

Baked Gloucester Haddock with Spicy Salsa de Juel

As a Mother's Day gift, two sisters who worked for us surprised us with a traditional Latin feast inspired by their upbringing in Guatemala. Knowing that Barbara had lived in Puerto Rico and that I love Latin food, they arrived with fried chicken, plátanos (plantains), habichuelas (beans), and arroz (rice).

The highlight was a flavorful, spicy sauce their brother Juel made to accompany the chicken. We loved it so much that we began serving it with haddock and rice. Every time we make this sauce, it reminds us of that special meal our friends delivered to us on Mother's Day, the busiest day of the year at the restaurant. We like local haddock for this dish, but you can substitute another white fish—or fried chicken!

Rice

1 cup jasmine rice

1 teaspoon kosher salt

Haddock

1 cup panko breadcrumbs

½ teaspoon kosher salt

½ teaspoon black pepper

½ teaspoon sweet paprika

½ cup extra-virgin olive oil, plus more for sautéing

4 haddock fillets (about 6 ounces each)

Sauce

2 tablespoons margarine (do not substitute butter)

1 small onion, finely diced

2 cups chopped tomatoes

1-2 small jalapeño peppers, finely diced (optional; remove seeds before dicing to lessen heat)

½ cup chicken broth

Salt and Pepper Mix (see recipe on page 54)

8 large shrimp, peeled and deveined

2 tablespoons dry vermouth

Garnish: ¼ cup chopped cilantro and quartered lime

Pepper

1. Cook rice:
   Rinse rice under cold water until the water runs clear. In a saucepan, bring 2 cups of water, rice, and salt to a boil. Reduce heat to low, cover, and simmer for 15 minutes. Remove from heat and let sit, covered, for at least 5 minutes. Fluff with a fork before serving.

2. Prepare haddock:
   Preheat oven to 375 degrees. Have a 9-inch by 13-inch baking dish ready. In medium bowl, combine panko, salt, pepper, and paprika. Pour olive oil in separate bowl. Quickly dip each haddock piece in olive oil, giving it a generous coating, and shake off any excess. Dredge haddock in seasoned panko, working quickly, put on a plate, and sprinkle with more panko.

Heat 2 tablespoons olive oil in oven-proof skillet over medium heat until almost smoking—it's important that the pan is hot! Tilt pan away from you slightly so oil pools in the lower area, then slide haddock gently into the pan. Return the pan to level and shake it back and forth a couple times to spread the oil under the fish. Sauté until you see edges browning, about 4 minutes. If crust is not sticking to the fish, increase heat slightly. Flip haddock over and sauté until crispy around the edges. If needed, cook the fish in batches to avoid crowding the pan, adding more oil when needed.

Transfer skillet to oven and bake for 15-20 minutes, or until haddock is opaque and flakes easily with a fork. If you don't have an oven-proof skillet, transfer haddock to baking dish before putting into oven.

Baked Gloucester Haddock Variation without Crispy Panko

Instead of step 2, preheat oven to 400 degrees. Place haddock in 9-inch by 13-inch baking dish, sprinkle with salt, pepper, and paprika, and drizzle with 2-3 tablespoons white wine and 2-3 tablespoons extra-virgin olive oil. Pour ¼ cup water into pan. Bake 12-15 minutes, until the fish flakes easily and is opaque, basting with the olive oil and wine halfway through.

3. Make Salsa de Juel:
   In a medium-size saucepan, melt margarine over medium heat. Add onion and sauté until translucent, about 3-4 minutes. Stir in tomatoes and jalapeño. Season with salt and pepper. Pour in chicken broth and simmer for 10-12 minutes, stirring occasionally, until the mixture thickens into a chunky salsa. Set aside.

4. Sauté shrimp:
   Heat 1 tablespoon olive oil in skillet over medium heat. Add shrimp, sprinkle with pinch of salt, and cook for 1-2 minutes per side until opaque. Add vermouth and let it reduce for about 1 minute. Stir in 2 tablespoons of Salsa de Juel and simmer for another minute.

5. Plate the haddock and sauce:
   Divide rice onto plates. Place haddock fillets on rice. Spoon Salsa de Juel generously over the haddock. Top with sautéed shrimp, cilantro, a squeeze of fresh lime (if desired), and serve.

SERVES 4

Baked Scallop, Shrimp, and Artichoke Skewers

A My Place signature entrée. It was featured in a Friends of Dana-Farber Cancer Institute cookbook and chosen to be paired with two other chefs' recipes as part of a spring menu. The mustard panko creates a crispy crunch that is perfect with the seafood and artichoke.

½ cup Dijon mustard

6 large shrimp (U-15—15 or fewer shrimp per pound); we like to keep tails on for appearance and flavor

6 scallops (10-20 per-pound size)

4 large canned whole artichoke hearts, drained

1 ¼ cups panko breadcrumbs

2 tablespoons melted butter

3 tablespoons extra-virgin olive oil, divided

2 wooden skewers soaked in water

1. Prepare skewers:
   Preheat oven to 450 degrees and choose convection if available. Place mustard, shrimp, and scallops in large bowl and toss to coat evenly. Put panko into another large bowl.

   Thread a shrimp onto skewer through the tail and middle section so it curls, then thread a scallop through the middle, then an artichoke heart, and continue, alternating with shrimp, scallop, and artichoke. Thread another skewer with the alternating shrimp, scallop, and artichoke hearts. Roll skewers in panko.

2. Bake skewers:
   Add butter and 2 tablespoons olive oil to small rimmed baking sheet and put in the oven 2 minutes to heat. Place the skewers on sheet and drizzle with 1 tablespoon olive oil.

   Bake until golden brown on top and cooked through, about 8-10 minutes or longer, depending on oven temperature.

3. Serve:
   Turn the golden crispy sides of the shrimp, scallop, and artichokes facing up on plate and remove the skewers.

SERVES 2

Sesame Herb-Crusted Tuna with Sweet Pepper Slaw

When we have access to sushi-grade tuna, we love to encrust it with sesame seeds and pan sear both sides to form a nice crust while the inside remains rare. A colorful pepper slaw, with a spicy orange soy sauce and steamed jasmine rice makes for a dramatic presentation.

Rice

½ cup jasmine rice

Spicy orange soy sauce

1 ¼ cups orange marmalade

1-2 tablespoons of sambal, depending on your heat preference (you can substitute spicy chili sauce or Sriracha)

¾ cup soy sauce

¼ cup white wine

½ cup julienned combination of red, orange, and yellow peppers

½ cup julienned English cucumbers

¼ cup julienned carrots

Sesame crust

¼ cup chopped cilantro (wash and shake dry all herbs before chopping)

¼ cup chopped parsley

¼ cup chopped basil

1 tablespoon chopped shallots

½ tablespoon chopped garlic

2 tablespoons toasted sesame seeds

2 tablespoons peanut oil

1 tablespoon sesame oil

Pinch **Salt and Pepper Mix** (see recipe on page 54)

Tuna

2 7-ounce sushi-grade tuna fillets

1 tablespoon peanut oil

1 tablespoon sesame oil

Garnishes

Gomashio (Japanese seasoning with equal parts toasted, crushed sesame seeds and sea salt), optional

Wasabi, if desired

1. Steam rice:
   Cook rice according to package instructions.

2. Mix slaw:
   In large bowl, combine marmalade, sambal, soy sauce, and white wine. Remove ½ cup of sauce and set aside. To the remaining sauce, add peppers, cucumbers, and carrots and toss to combine. Set aside.

3. Prepare tuna crust:
   On a dinner plate, add all sesame crust ingredients and mix well. Press tuna fillets, one at a time, into the crust mixture, flip, and press again.

4. Sear tuna fillets:
   Heat heavy-bottom sauté pan on high for 2 minutes. Add peanut oil and sesame oil, and when smoking hot, carefully place tuna in pan and press down to evenly sear crust. Once underside is golden brown, flip and repeat, searing 3-4 minutes each side, depending on thickness and preferred temperature. Remove tuna from pan and place on cutting board.

5. Plate tuna and slaw:
Slice tuna against the grain in wide strips so that you see the ruby color of the rare tuna contrasting with the seared outside. On each plate, spoon a line of jasmine rice on one side, then place tuna strips about a half inch apart, and roll tuna over rice, tucking the pieces around the rice to make little roulades.

6. Place the reserved orange sauce in the sauté pan to heat it. Spoon sauce over tuna slices and around plate. Mound pepper slaw in the center and sprinkle some around the tuna. Finish with a generous sprinkle of gomashio, about 1 tablespoon on each plate, and serve with wasabi if desired.

SERVES 2

Portuguese Fisherman's Stew

Some people would say this soulful, show-stopping stew is the most flavorful recipe in this book. A nod to Nantucket's deep Portuguese roots, it began as a pot of Couves—a traditional vegetable soup made with kale, potatoes, and linguica. Then Kathy made a fresh seafood version, using the pristine trimmings from fillets of halibut, salmon, and swordfish, along with mussels, shrimp, and sometimes scallops—whatever the day's catch offered. She also used San Marzano tomatoes, crushed red pepper, and herbs to pick up the flavor. This, along with the linguica, gives it the fiery broth. The result was a rich, vibrant dish that's full of flavor.

Years ago, *Gourmet* magazine called to request the recipe. And still, longtime guests come through the door asking for it. Many people tell us they've never tried any other dishes because they only want to enjoy this when they come to the restaurant. Bonus: It's naturally gluten-free.

2 tablespoons extra-virgin olive oil

3 ½ ounces linguica sausage, cut in ¼-inch or thinner half-moon slices

12 ounces skinless salmon cut into 8 pieces (you can substitute haddock)

8 shrimp (size U-15, about 15 shrimp per pound)

8 sea scallops (size 10/20, 10-20 scallops per pound)

1 tablespoon chopped garlic

1 tablespoon chopped shallots

1 leek, white and light green parts thinly sliced

½ teaspoon crushed red pepper (use 1 teaspoon if you like more heat)

1 tablespoon herbs de Provence (make sure it includes tarragon!)

Salt and Pepper Mix (see recipe on page 54)

½ cup dry white vermouth

2 cups clam juice

4 ounces cleaned mussels or littleneck clams

1 ¼ cups diced tomatoes in juice or canned San Marzano whole tomatoes in juice (break up the tomatoes with your hands)

Cooked potato, pasta, or rice (optional)

Garnish: Cilantro sprigs (optional)

1. Warm olive oil in large wok-style pan or large saucepan over medium-high heat. Add linguica and sear until lightly browned. Add salmon, shrimp, scallops, and mussels (or clams) and do not stir. If using haddock, add that later so it doesn't break apart.

2. Top the seafood with the garlic, shallots, leeks, crushed red pepper, and herbs de Provence. Season with salt and pepper and do not stir. Cook for about 3 minutes, giving the seafood a chance to sear before you add the liquid. Add vermouth and shake pan back and forth to distribute it. Stir in clam juice and tomato sauce, scrape the bottom of the pan with the spoon to release the bits that stick, turn down heat to medium, and if using haddock, add it, and cover the pan.

Simmer until seafood is cooked through, about 7 minutes. If needed, add more clam juice or tomatoes to adjust consistency. Taste broth, and add more salt and pepper, and crushed red pepper if needed. If desired, add cooked potato chunks, pasta, or rice.

3. Serve in bowls and garnish with cilantro.

SERVES 4 FOR DINNER OR 6-8 AS AN APPETIZER

Lobster Tacos

When the *Phantom Gourmet* television show visited the restaurant, they declared, "Of everything on the menu, the best dish might be the signature My Place Lobster Taco."

A few things to know: It's not the kind of taco you pick up with your hands. It's a fork-and-knife taco, and its dramatic presentation never fails to turn heads in the dining room. One food writer even called our lobster tacos more photogenic than the iconic Motif No. 1!

This dish originated when we set out to create another signature lobster item. Our popular lobster quesadilla took up so much space in our oven, and we realized a lobster taco would be a perfect option—especially for our tiny kitchen.

The flavor profile starts with sweet, freshly grilled lobster, lightly seasoned with Old Bay, tucked into a crispy corn tortilla that we fry up fresh. A chiffonade of Napa cabbage adds a refreshing crunch, and a dollop of chipotle mayo brings just the right tangy kick. It's a spectacular way to showcase lobster—hearty yet light, and naturally gluten-free.

Kate Capshaw became a fan while filming "The Love Letter" in Rockport. She and her family celebrated her son Theo's 10th birthday on our upstairs deck, enjoying—yes—these very lobster tacos. One night, the restaurant was so full we even had to (regretfully!) turn her away.

We make our own taco shells shaped into a floret to hold the cabbage and lobster filling. If you are short on time, you can use premade taco shells, but they will not hold as much filling and will not be as attractive.

6 ounces freshly shucked, cooked lobster meat (tail, knuckle, and claw) (if cooking your own lobster, you'll need a 1 ½- to 2-pound lobster)

Old Bay Olive Oil Mix (see recipe on page 55)

2 6-inch yellow corn tortillas

Canola oil for frying

Salt and Pepper Mix (see recipe on page 54)

About 3 tablespoons **Chipotle Mayonnaise** (see recipe on page 54)

3 cups shredded Napa cabbage

2 tablespoons chopped scallions

2 tablespoons chopped heirloom cherry tomatoes

Garnish: Cilantro sprigs (optional)

1. Make the shells:
   Line large plate with paper towels. In a medium saucepan or deep fryer, add enough oil to submerge a tortilla. Heat to 375 degrees or until oil is hot enough for frying. Place one tortilla at a time in the oil and submerge it. Use a ladle to press down on the center of the tortilla so the bottom sits flat and the edges curl around the ladle to make a floret, or cup shape, and count 15 seconds. Remove ladle and continue frying tortilla until golden brown, about 3-4 minutes. Transfer to prepared plate and season generously with salt and pepper. Repeat with second tortilla.

2. Prepare the lobster:
   Pour 1 tablespoon Old Bay Olive Oil Mix into small bowl. Heat grill, grill pan, or skillet to medium-high heat. Dip each lobster piece into Old Bay mix, shake off excess, and grill or pan-sear briefly to warm lobster. Transfer to plate and set aside.

3. Assemble tacos:
   Place dollop of chipotle mayonnaise on the center of two dinner plates and place taco shells on mayonnaise (this holds it in place). Fill tortillas with shredded cabbage, then top with scallions, tomatoes, and a good dollop of the chipotle mayonnaise. Place grilled lobster decoratively on top and garnish with fresh cilantro.

MAKES 2 TACOS, 1 ENTRÉE OR 2 APPETIZER SERVINGS

Grilled Barbecue Scallops with Sweet Potato Purée

While the combination of scallops with sweet potatoes may seem unusual, it's a pleasing contrast of textures and smoky, sweet, and savory flavors. Lacquering scallops with barbecue sauce gives them richness that plays nicely with a silky sweet potato mash and earthy mushrooms. A drizzle of maple-soy vinaigrette ties it all together.

3 medium sweet potatoes

2 tablespoons unsalted butter

2 tablespoons brown sugar

2 tablespoons maple syrup

Salt and Pepper Mix (see recipe on page 54)

½ cup **Maple Soy Vinaigrette** (see recipe on page 50), divided, plus more for drizzling

3 large white or oyster mushrooms, sliced (about 2 cups)

8-12 large scallops (U-10 size, which is less than 10 scallops per pound)

Extra-virgin olive oil (if pan sautéeing)

¼ cup **Barbecue Sauce** (see recipe on page 53)

Organic vegetables such as haricot verts, zucchini, and summer squash for serving

1. Prepare sweet potatoes:
   Peel sweet potatoes, cut into 2 ½-inch chunks, put in large saucepan, cover with water, and boil until fork tender. Once cool enough to handle, mash with butter, sugar, and maple syrup. Season with salt and pepper. Taste and adjust seasoning so that it's slightly sweet but not overly sweet. Set aside.

2. Grill or sauté mushrooms:
   Toss mushrooms with ¼ cup vinaigrette. Shake off excess and grill or sauté them in a small skillet on medium-high heat until cooked through. Set aside.

3. Grill or sauté scallops:
   Preheat oven to 400 degrees. Toss scallops with ¼ cup vinaigrette. To grill (which gives them attractive grill marks): Shake excess liquid off scallops and grill 2-3 minutes per side, using a spatula to turn them over. Remove from grill and transfer to oven-safe skillet. To pan sauté: Heat medium oven-safe skillet over high heat and add a tablespoon of olive oil. Shake excess liquid off scallops and place in pan, cooking in batches if needed to avoid crowding them. Cook 1-2 minutes per side until firm and nicely seared with golden brown edges. Cooking time depends on the size of the scallops.

4. Finish scallops in oven:
   Brush scallops with barbecue sauce and slide skillet in the oven for 3-4 minutes to lacquer the barbecue sauce.

5. Plate the scallops and sweet potatoes:
   Divide mashed sweet potatoes onto four plates. Top with mushrooms and place one scallop on mushrooms and remaining scallops around sweet potatoes. Drizzle with pan juices and extra vinaigrette and serve with organic vegetables.

MAKES 4 ENTRÉE SERVINGS

Sautéed Lobster in Sherry Butter with Conchiglie Pasta

We love the indulgence of tender lobster bathed in a sherry butter cream sauce and tossed with seashell pasta. The vegetables in the recipe shift with the seasons: Tomato Basil Corn Salad in summer, sweet butternut squash in fall, and peas with mushrooms in spring.

1 pound good-quality conchiglie (seashell) or orecchiette pasta (We only use imported De Cecco brand pasta)

1 tablespoon extra-virgin olive oil, plus more for garnish

1 teaspoon chopped shallots

1 cup thinly sliced leek rings

½ cup cream sherry

1 cup **Tomato Basil Corn Salad** (see recipe on page 76), or 1 cup butternut squash cut into ⅛-inch cubes and steamed or roasted, or 1 cup cooked peas and mushrooms

½ cup lobster stock or chicken broth

4 tablespoons unsalted butter

½ cup heavy cream

¼ grated Asiago cheese

½ cup halved heirloom cherry tomatoes

12 ounces to 1 pound cooked lobster meat (tail, knuckle, and claw)

¼ cup chopped basil

Salt and Pepper Mix (see recipe on page 54)

¼ cup chopped flat-leaf parsley for garnish

Sea salt

Freshly ground pepper

1. Cook pasta:
   Follow package instructions to cook pasta al dente. Drain and set aside.

2. Prepare sauce:
   Add oil to wok-style pan or large skillet and heat to medium. Sauté shallots and leeks for about 1 ½ minutes, stirring and watching carefully to avoid browning. Add sherry and simmer for 2 minutes.

3. Stir in Tomato Basil Corn Salad (or vegetable of choice), lobster stock, butter, cream, cheese, and tomatoes, and simmer until sauce thickens slightly, about 4 minutes. Add lobster and chopped basil and season with salt and pepper. Toss with cooked pasta until pasta is warm, but do not overcook.

4. Plate pasta:
   Using a slotted spoon, transfer pasta and lobster to four plates, leaving the sauce in the pan. Further reduce sauce for another minute and then pour over pasta. Top each serving with parsley, drizzle of extra-virgin olive oil (about 1 teaspoon), and sprinkle of sea salt and freshly ground pepper.

SERVES 4

Lobster Ravioli with Brandy Cream Sauce

This comment from our recipe tester says it all: "The flavors were PHENOMENAL. This will be my new 'I really want to impress these people' recipe. The filling is balanced and creamy, and the brandy cream sauce is decadent without being heavy."

Pasta dough

1 12-ounce jar roasted red peppers, drained

2 eggs, plus 1 egg whisked with 1 tablespoon water for egg wash

1 teaspoon extra-virgin olive oil

2 ½-3 ½ cups all-purpose flour, plus more for shaping dough

Filling

1 egg

15 ounces ricotta cheese

1 teaspoon extra-virgin olive oil

6 ounces freshly shucked, cooked lobster meat (tail, knuckle, and claw), roughly chopped (shrimp, crab, or a mixture work well too)

¼ cup finely chopped basil leaves

Salt and Pepper Mix (see recipe on page 54)

Brandy Cream Sauce

Garnishes

Grana, Pecorino Romano, or Parmigiano Reggiano cheese

Fresh basil

High-quality, extra-virgin olive oil (optional)

Special equipment required: Pasta machine

1. Make pasta dough:
   Purée red peppers in food processor, making sure no pepper pieces remain. Add 2 eggs and olive oil and process until combined. Add flour, ½ cup at a time, and process, scraping down sides of the bowl to ensure dough is well mixed. Remove dough from processor, roll in flour to form a ball, adding more flour if dough is too sticky to handle. Wrap in plastic and let rest in refrigerator for 30 minutes.

2. Prepare filling:
   Beat 1 egg in large bowl. Stir in ricotta cheese and season with salt and pepper. Add Grana cheese and mix well. Stir in lobster, basil, and another pinch of salt and pepper. Refrigerate filling.

3. Form ravioli sheets:
   Place pasta dough on floured surface and cut into three pieces. Pinch or roll out each piece with rolling pin until dough is thin enough to pass through pasta machine. Crank pasta through machine twice on "1" setting, once on "2" setting, and once on "3" setting, adding flour as needed to work dough through the machine. Repeat with remaining dough. The pasta sheets should be roughly 5 inches wide and 18 to 24 inches long. Cover pasta sheets with a damp towel so they don't dry out while you are rolling out dough and forming ravioli.

4. Form and fill ravioli:
   Cut dough sheets in half so each piece measures about 5 inches wide and between 9 to 12 inches long. Trim edges with a knife so they are straight. Brush both sheets with egg wash. On one dough sheet, starting 1 inch from the short edge, place about 2 teaspoons of filling in the centerline, then place 5 dollops of filling about 1 inch apart from each other. Take care to avoid overfilling ravioli; you need a border around the filling so the

pasta doesn't stretch and tear. Top with another sheet, placing egg wash side face down. Press on edges to seal ravioli.

Cut each ravioli, leaving about 1 inch on each side of the filling. Raviolis will be about 4-inch by 4-inch squares. Use a fork to crimp all four sides of each ravioli. If not cooking right away, store in the refrigerator for up to two days or freeze.

5. Prepare Brandy Cream Sauce (recipe below).

6. Cook ravioli:
Bring large pot of salted water to boil. Have plate or bowl set aside. Carefully drop in ravioli. Once they rise to the top, cook for another 3-4 minutes. Remove cooked ravioli and transfer to plate or bowl.

7. Plate ravioli:
Serve two large ravioli per person, spooning sauce, vegetables, and remaining lobster on top. Garnish each with two basil leaves and a sprinkle of cheese. Finish with a drizzle of good-quality, extra-virgin olive oil, if desired.

MAKES 14-16 4-INCH-SQUARE RAVIOLI. SERVES 6-8 AS AN ENTRÉE.

Brandy Cream Sauce

1 tablespoon extra-virgin olive oil

1 tablespoon minced shallots

¼ cup thinly sliced leek rings

¾ cup brandy

½ cup lobster stock or chicken broth

1 cup heavy cream

½ cup grated Grana, Pecorino Romano, or Parmigiano Reggiano cheese

Salt and Pepper Mix (see recipe on page 54)

4 ounces freshly shucked, cooked lobster, divided (use half in sauce and the remainder for garnish)

1 cup chopped vegetables (we like thinly sliced matchsticks of zucchini, carrots, and summer squash for the colors, contrast, and toothsome texture, but you also can use tomatoes, corn, peas, and mushrooms)

1. Prepare sauce:
Heat olive oil in medium saucepan over medium heat. Stir in shallots and leeks and sauté for about 1 minute until soft, being careful to avoid browning them. Turn off stove and remove pan from heat.

2. Add brandy, return pan to burner, and turn stove back to medium (brandy is flammable and this method avoids a flame up). Stir in lobster stock or chicken broth, heavy cream, and cheese, and season with salt and pepper. Stir constantly while sauce reduces, about 3-4 minutes. Add lobster and vegetables and further reduce sauce so it's creamy but not too thick, about 3-4 minutes. If the sauce doesn't seem like it will be enough to coat the ravioli with extra to drizzle on the plate, add additional stock and heavy cream. Taste and add more salt and pepper if needed. Keep sauce warm until ready to serve.

The Colonel's Dinner that Wasn't

One day, many years ago, we ran into our friend Jennifer McCarthy while she was walking her dog. At the time, her husband Donald "Mac" McCarthy, a retired Colonel in the Marines, was having some health issues. He was a big guy, with a big personality and a commanding presence.

When we heard that Mac was under the weather, we said, "Hey, would you like us to send over dinner tonight?"

She lit up. "Oh, that would be lovely," she said in her British accent.

I asked if they'd like the Grilled Barbecue Scallops with Sweet Potato Purée, one of their favorites. She was thrilled.

"I'll tell Mac. He'll be so excited."

"What time?" I asked.

"Six o'clock," she said, very precisely.

"Perfect," I said. "We'll have it there at six."

I got to work, typed a little note into the computer—"Send dinner to Jennifer"—and went on with the day. It was summer, with a chaotic rush of nonstop cooking that day.

Fast forward to 10 p.m. Barbara came upstairs and said, "Did you ever send dinner to Jennifer?" I froze and I just went pale. "No... no, I didn't."

I called Jennifer immediately, completely mortified.

"Jennifer, I am so, so sorry."

And with that very calm, British voice she said, "Well... we made our gin and tonics at 5:45... and we sat. And we waited. And waited. And kept peeking out the front door. But alas... no dinner."

I was horrified. This is the Colonel's wife. This was a highly decorated and revered Colonel and I completely dropped the ball! It took me years to live it down (it's still taking me years). Every time I saw her, I was reminded of that night. You don't leave a Colonel and his wife waiting for dinner. Punished for life! —Kath

Grilled Salmon with Grapefruit and Beet Salad with Poppyseed Vinaigrette

When we created this main-dish salad for our Paleo and gluten-free friends, we wanted it to taste as good as it looks. Jewel-toned beets, ruby red grapefruit, orange Sumos, and heirloom tomatoes bring a burst of color against crisp greens and grilled salmon. A drizzle of poppyseed vinaigrette adds brightness while making the plate even more eye-catching.

4 medium- to large-size mix of Chioggia and golden beets

1 teaspoon chopped garlic

4 6-ounce skin-on salmon fillets

Old Bay Olive Oil Mix (see recipe on page 55)

1 ruby red grapefruit, peeled and cut into segments

1-2 Sumo or mandarin oranges, cut into segments

8 cups (about 4 ounces) salad greens of your choice

Handful chopped heirloom tomatoes or other flavorful tomatoes

Spiced Pecans (see recipe on page 56)

Poppyseed Vinaigrette (see recipe on page 50)

1. Roast beets:
   Preheat oven to 450 degrees. Wash beets and place in roasting pan with garlic and water to fill 1 inch of the pan. Cover with foil and roast until a knife easily pierces beets, about 1 hour or longer (cooking time depends on size of beets). Once beets are cool enough to handle, peel and slice.

2. Cook salmon:
   Dip salmon in Old Bay Olive Oil Mix and grill (our preference) or pan-sear, cooking to your preferred level of doneness. If poaching salmon, brush with Old Bay Olive Oil Mix after cooking.

3. Plate salads:
   Divide lettuce onto plates. Arrange beets, grapefruit and orange segments, tomatoes, and spiced pecans on plates and top with the grilled salmon. Drizzle dressing over salad and onto plate so poppyseeds are visible.

SERVES 4

Bolognese

Hearty, slow-simmered, and brimming with rich flavor, this Bolognese is made for gathering with friends or family. A mix of ground beef, sweet Italian sausage, Chianti, and plenty of My Place Tomato Sauce cooks down into a luscious sauce that only gets better when made a day ahead. The recipe makes enough to feed a crowd and is also freezer-friendly. This recipe is a fan favorite of our good friend Ken Novack.

Sauce

6 tablespoons extra-virgin olive oil

1 teaspoon chopped garlic (1 medium-size clove)

2 medium-size carrots, peeled and finely diced

1 stalk celery, finely diced

½ large onion, finely diced

2 teaspoons dried basil leaves

1 teaspoon dried oregano

1 pound ground beef

1 pound sweet Italian sausage removed from casing

1 ½ cups dry red wine, preferably Chianti

7 cups **My Place Tomato Sauce** (see recipe on page 57; triple the recipe)

Parmesan cheese rind (optional)

Salt and Pepper Mix (see recipe on page 54)

For serving

Extra-virgin olive oil

Pasta (we like imported De Cecco conchiglie or large shells, cooked in well-salted water until al dente); use 6 ounces per serving

Freshly grated cheese, such as Grana

Fresh basil, chopped

1. Prepare sauce:

In large pot over medium-high heat, warm olive oil. Stir in garlic and add carrots, celery, onion, basil, and oregano. Season with salt and pepper. Sauté 5 minutes, being careful to avoid browning the vegetables; add extra oil if necessary. Season with salt and pepper.

Add ground beef and sausage, breaking them apart with two large spoons using criss-cross motion until pieces are small. Season with salt and pepper and add wine. Simmer until wine is reduced by about half, about 15 to 20 minutes. Skim excess oil or fat off top.

Mix in My Place Tomato Sauce and reduce heat to medium. Add cheese rind if using. Simmer about 45 minutes, stirring every 5 to 10 minutes. Sauce is done when vegetables are soft. Taste sauce and adjust seasoning as needed.

2. Serve:

Cook pasta according to package instructions.

If you made the sauce the previous day, heat one cup of sauce per serving in saucepan. Toss pasta with sauce. If it's thicker than you would like, add 1 tablespoon chicken stock or water to thin.

Divide pasta onto plates, top each with a drizzle of extra-virgin olive oil, 1 teaspoon grated cheese, and chopped fresh basil. If desired, top with additional My Place Tomato Sauce.

SERVES 8-10; MAKES ABOUT 8 CUPS

Chicken Milanese

One of our Hump Day regulars, Beth Zerilli, craved this dish all throughout COVID, when we weren't allowed to serve customers in the restaurant. She ordered it regularly for her family to enjoy at home, and even now, if it's missing from the menu, she'll ask the server: "Where is the Chicken Milanese?" Simple, comforting, and delicious—this dish has earned its place as a favorite.

Toppings

16 red bliss potatoes

1 tablespoon extra-virgin olive oil

16 pieces prosciutto

2 tablespoons or more canola oil

Sea salt

Chicken

4 eggs

1 cup all-purpose flour

3 ½ cups panko breadcrumbs

2 cups Asiago or other grated cheese

4 8-ounce boneless, skinless chicken breasts (size of chicken breasts can vary)

2 tablespoons or more extra-virgin olive oil

Salad

10 ounces arugula

1-2 lemons

8 tablespoons good-quality extra-virgin olive oil

1 ½ cups halved cherry tomatoes, preferably heirloom

24 pitted Kalamata olives

24 or more shaved Asiago cheese strips (make using a vegetable peeler)

4 avocados, sliced

1. Prepare potatoes:
   Fill medium saucepan with 2 inches of water, place steamer basket in pot, add potatoes, and cover. Bring to a boil, reduce heat to medium, and steam until potatoes can be pierced with a fork, about 15-20 minutes. Remove potatoes and let cool, then slice, brush with olive oil, sprinkle with sea salt, and grill or broil until nicely browned. Set aside to cool.

2. Make crispy prosciutto:
   Line plate with paper towels. Heat 2 tablespoons canola oil in medium skillet over medium-high heat. Fry prosciutto in batches, about 2-3 minutes per side until golden brown and crispy, and transfer to plate to cool. Add more oil as needed between batches.

3. Prepare chicken:
   Preheat oven to 425 degrees. In a large bowl, whisk eggs with ¼ cup water. Place flour in second large bowl. In a third large bowl, combine panko and cheese.

   Cut each chicken piece in half horizontally, so they are half their thickness, then pound with a mallet or heavy skillet until ⅛-inch thick. Coat each chicken breast in flour, shake off excess, dip in egg wash, shake off excess, and coat in panko, patting it in. Repeat with remaining chicken breasts. Sprinkle the top of each with extra panko and cheese mixture. (You may end up with extra coating, but you want to make sure you have extra so the coating doesn't get sticky.)

Have rimmed baking sheet ready. Heat large skillet with 2 tablespoons olive oil over medium-high heat and add chicken breasts in batches to avoid overcrowding. Cook until crispy and golden brown and flip over to crisp other side. Add oil as needed between batches. Transfer cooked chicken to rimmed baking sheet and finish cooking in the oven for 5-7 minutes. Cut one piece in the center to check doneness.

4. Plate salads:
Divide arugula onto eight plates and dress with a squeeze of fresh lemon and drizzle of good-quality extra-virgin olive oil. Top with halved cherry tomatoes, crispy prosciutto pieces, olives, cheese, avocado slices, and potato slices. Place chicken on top, and squeeze fresh lemon juice over chicken and around lettuce.

SERVES 8

Chapter 5

Through the Years

"You Girls"

It was a huge win for the Rockport hockey team, having made it into the state tournament for the first time in 10 years. On that Sunday afternoon, the game was close, and the crowd and team went wild as the clock ticked down to the final seconds to the win.

Barb turned to Kath and said, "We gotta go celebrate somewhere. I'll call Peter and Sammy and see if they can take us at their trattoria in the West End."

Barb called Peter and said, "We won! We'd like to come for pizza. Can you take us?"

"Sure, how many will it be?" Peter asked.

"About 50-60 in about 20 minutes," Barb said casually.

At that, Peter exclaimed, "WHAT!!! YOU GIRLS!!"

Hockey Team Dinners

The Rockport hockey team is comprised of players from three neighboring towns as well as Rockport. One of our employees played on the team, and when it came time for his family to host the traditional team dinner, they weren't in a position to take it on. We stepped in and offered to host the dinner at a centrally located restaurant where everyone could gather.

That first year, the turnout was modest, about 20 players and their dads. But it quickly became a tradition. Each year, the event grew, and soon it became the occasion where we presented the varsity jackets we sponsored. By the fifth year, the dinner had swelled to nearly 100 people! Families came with grandmothers, aunts, and younger siblings in tow. Their little sisters even started their own tradition of enjoying tea parties in the back room while the older kids celebrated.

One of our favorite memories was snapping a photo of two Rockport High seniors proudly wearing their varsity jackets in the middle of the restaurant. We submitted the picture to the *Gloucester Daily Times*. We asked the restaurant owner if we could post a copy in their waiting area, alongside the other event photos on the wall. Her reply? "No. We don't like to endorse other businesses." Hmmm...

Taking Care of Teenagers in Our Community

When we discover someone in need, we try to step up. One of our young cooks, Paul, was struggling in high school. His school guidance counselor called us to say he was at risk of not graduating; could we do anything to help him along? We made an arrangement with him: Paul would clock into work early and get paid while meeting with the tutor we hired.

Then there was 15-year-old Rachel, lugging heavy baskets of wet laundry from King Street to the laundromat at Whistlestop because her family's dryer broke. We bought her a new clothes dryer.

We've also enjoyed celebrating our staff's milestones. For Michael's 16th birthday, we turned the upstairs dining room into a party space, complete with balloons, chicken and brie sandwiches, and cake for him and seven friends. His mom was traveling in Spain and couldn't be there, so we made sure he felt celebrated.

Another birthday celebration was for Hannah. When we asked if she had birthday plans, she said no. So of course, we made some. Thirty guests, lobster ravioli, Caesar salad, and a birthday cake later, Hannah had quite the celebration. Adding to the fun, a staff member dressed as Elvis in a white jumpsuit and sang happy birthday, Elvis style. We guess she did have quite the plan!

An Oasis of Culinary Love and Humanity

The spark and magic of My Place by the Sea sprouts from the kindness of the owners who put the well-being of others—from their staff to their customers—foremost in all that they do. They've nurtured generations of teens who come through their doors, often naïve to the rigors of the workplace. A stint at the restaurant transforms them into young adults who can make their way in the world and find success in an increasingly complex world. Kathy and Barb go above and beyond. When an employee

needs support or guidance from an adult in their life, they step up. When a customer appears with a living or a dying wish, they show up. They always show up, and the world is a better place for it.

— Gail McCarthy
   Gloucester Daily Times
   reporter

It's All Good

We decided to buy Melissa a car. She had been working for us since she was 14. Now at 18, Melissa was living on her own, totally self-sufficient. Melissa was diligent, quiet, and a model employee who never complained or asked for any special favors.

Most employees were dropped off at the restaurant front door or drove cars their parents had given them and parked in front of the restaurant. Our friends Steven Law and his husband Donald Stroud told us they saw Melissa taking a bus from Pigeon Cove, carrying her pressed button-down white shirt and tie on a hanger, to get to work each day. When we heard that, we knew we had to get her a car and that it had to be a new one so she wouldn't have to worry.

So, one afternoon, we stepped away from the restaurant to go car shopping, leaving the crew in charge. After some time at the car dealership, Barb thought she'd better check in. She called Melissa who reported, "Well, we had a power outage, so we had to close the restaurant." Barb calmly ended the call.

Kath looked over and said, "So, how's everything at the restaurant?" Barb replied: "It's perfect." So, we continued shopping.

When Hollywood Came to Bearskin Neck

One afternoon, we received a call with a special request: Ellen DeGeneres and Anne Heche wanted to dine with us that evening. Ellen herself called and said, "Everywhere we go, we cause a commotion. Could you seat us away from a crowd, somewhere quiet?" Of course, we said yes and planned to seat them on the upper deck. This was when "The Love Letter" was being filmed in Rockport.

But here's the funny part: When Ellen and Anne arrived at the front door, the first people they encountered were Ellen's boss at the time, Mr. Hollywood, Steven Spielberg, with Kate Capshaw and their family, seated in a highly public spot near the entrance. They hadn't asked for any special treatment and were completely unconcerned about being in plain view of the public. Hmmm...

Kathy's Brother, Mike Milbury

While Mike served as general manager of the New York Islanders hockey team, he and his family often visited us even though we were Bruins fans at heart.

For those who don't follow sports, here's some background. Mike is a National Hockey League legend and Hall of Famer from his 12 seasons with the Boston Bruins from 1975 to 1987. After retiring as a player, he became assistant general manager and head coach for the Bruins, and later, general manager and head coach for the Islanders. He has a loyal, highly enthusiastic fan base in both regions, which tend to be archrivals in multiple sports.

One year, while the NHL draft was taking place at the Boston Garden, Mike brought the entire Islanders' coaching staff to the restaurant for dinner. Before their arrival, the team sent us an abundance of Islanders swag: hats, t-shirts, etc. That night, all of us were decked out in our new gear like superfans, much to the confusion of our customers. Many wondered why we were showing support for a New York team. We had to explain that the Islanders' coaching staff was dining on the upper deck, relaxing after a Gloucester booze cruise.

Max, one of our young servers and himself a serious athlete, could barely contain his enthusiasm for meeting Mike. When we introduced them, Max blurted out, "So nice to meet you, Mike. Who do you think you'll pick tomorrow at the draft?!" To which Mike replied, "[expletive expletive], I'm not telling you! You'll tell Harry Sinden!" Sinden was the Bruins longtime general manager and a competitor. At that point, Mike turned and walked away to join his colleagues. Kath reassured Max, "You never know what Mike will say." Max just laughed, exclaiming, "That was awesome! That was the best thing ever!" For that moment, he felt like a fellow athlete.

Slick Rick

Mike and the Stanley Cup Ring

Mike celebrated his 60th birthday in 2012 in unforgettable style at My Place. He, his wife, and six children began the celebration at a Rockport vacation home just a short walk from the restaurant. A bagpiper then led the family's procession down Bearskin Neck to My Place. When they arrived at the restaurant, the bagpiper played "Ave Maria" outside, serenading them as they filed onto the upstairs deck where they could still listen.

We were delighted to celebrate Mike's birthday with him, and thrilled by what he'd recently been given: a Stanley Cup ring! The previous year, the Bruins won the Stanley Cup against the Vancouver Canucks. As part of the "Bruins family" and an NECN announcer, Mike was given one of the precious rings in the same manner as the players. The funny thing was that Mike was super casual about owning it. Perhaps it would have carried more meaning if he had received it for playing or coaching the Bruins. When someone asked, "Where's the ring?" He replied, "Oh, I forgot. It's on the mantle of the house on King Street. Send the busser to go grab it!"

That's when our 15-year-old busser, "Slick Rick," sprang into action. He said, "I have my skateboard. I'll go get it!" And off he skated to retrieve the $40,000 diamond ring as Mike instructed, "The door's open. It's on the fireplace mantle."

What should have been a 15-minute skateboard ride took one hour. Along the way, the teenager stopped at every shop and person to show off the prized ring that he was cool enough to have in his possession.

Later that night, Mike left the ring with the Rockport Police because they wanted to see it. He told them, "Just drop it off with the girls at the restaurant." During the following days, the Stanley Cup ring made its way around Rockport and all of Cape Ann to the delight of everyone who got to try it on and snap a photo. Thanks, Mike!

The Water Rescue

Late in the day on an October afternoon, the National Weather Service issued a wind and surf advisory for Sandy Bay and nearby areas—the waterfront restaurant's side and front yards. Peering out the restaurant windows, we could see the now whitecapped bay getting rougher by the minute. Suddenly, Barb spotted a sailboat floundering in the turbulent waters. She immediately called Harbor Patrol.

As we watched from shore, three men clung to the bow as the boat ultimately capsized. One tried to swim to the shore, but the pounding waves and large rocks made it impossible. The swimmer was in trouble. That's when Henri, one of our dishwashers, followed by his brother Byron, went down to the rocks to help. Together, the brothers pulled the man ashore. During the rescue, many spectators gathered to witness the event and, of course, to take pictures.

Meanwhile, the Harbor Patrol arrived to collect the other two sailors and pull their boat to safe harbor. As it turned out, the sailors had been enjoying libations before the outing and ignored the weather warnings.

When we noticed the rescued swimmer shivering from his exposure to the frigid waters, we wrapped him in restaurant tablecloths to warm him up. He thanked the brothers profusely. Ironically, the man they saved was one of our staunch opponents when we worked to legalize the sale of alcohol in Rockport. Hmmm...

Local television stations and newspapers interviewed our heroic staff members. A local restaurant bought Byron and Henri champagne and swooned over them. They quit their jobs just a few weeks later. Perhaps the incident and the attention that came with it made them think they had a future in Hollywood.

The Early Days of COVID and the Bearskin Neck Ban

During the COVID pandemic, when the governor shut down all indoor and outdoor dining, restaurants were restricted to offering takeout only. The standard routine, as you may recall, went like this: Customers drove up to the restaurant, a server placed food in the trunk for "contactless" pickup, and everyone exchanged smiles and waves.

That was how it worked for all restaurants in this area except for one: My Place by the Sea.

Rockport's Board of Health imposed a restriction: Nonresidents were not allowed to enter Bearskin Neck, the nearly quarter-mile-long stretch leading to the restaurant. The board stated that the "narrow" road would force people to gather closer together and increase their risk. Less car traffic and fewer people walking on the street would help prevent disease spread, it was thought. This ruling was enforced by police stationed at the entrance of Bearskin Neck, questioning each pedestrian attempting to enter. As a result, My Place staff (thank you, Nick Hafey!) had to carry takeout orders down the entire Neck to nonresident customers waiting in Dock Square. On some days, Nick practically walked a marathon.

At the Board of Health meeting in which this decision was made, one member asked, "So, if I'm from Gloucester, I can't drive down Bearskin Neck to pick up dinner from My Place?" The answer: "That is correct." Meanwhile, a "resident" from anywhere in the world could pick up takeout from any other restaurant on any other street in town! Hmmm.

Through the Years

Dear Barbara....and Kathy.....

I am addressing this to you both after reading the introduction on your website... We...my wife Lotte along with George and Harriet Berkowitz have been on two occasions...been the recipients of your outstanding generosity.... I am writing to you to thank you for this extraordinary giving from the heart *that is the **positive energy*** along with the outstanding food....that makes "My Place By The Sea" so special... From my observation....this positive energy ....along with the food that is prepared with this same energy....is what makes your wonderful restaurant so very special... I recognize this energy....having preached it and recognized it as the key to what people need and hunger for!! Your restaurant....with its fabulous location.....is a restaurant with a fabulous location....nothing more....however it is the positive energy generated by you both ...that reaches the heart...that energizes people.....that is most essential and is what folks hunger for! I thank you for your generosity....for the delicious wonderful food....your outstanding staff that reflects your energy....and yesterday...Father's Day I was presented with a pair of Chef's Pants.....given by you....!!! I thank you both...for the special treatment....and for the POSITIVE ENERGY which you both have..... Today we rarely feel this energy and your demonstration....freely and naturally given by you both...is a reflection of who you are...and what you represent... Again....I THANK YOU BOTH.....the number of words we have exchanged over the visits to "My Place"...have been minimal....however your actions...and positive energy speak volumes.... Thank you for myself...my wife Lotte..and especially for my dear friends George and Harriet Berkowitz.....   Till next time...Bob Russo

GUESS WHAT DAY IT IS?!

The DOUBLE BULL
TAPHOUSE • GRILL

Thursday, April 3, 2025

Chef Kathy Milbury and Barbara Stavropoulos
68 Bearskin Neck
Rockport, MA 01966

Dear Kathy and Barbara,

From all of us here at Double Bull, **congratulations on an incredible 25 years!**
As all of us know all too well, running a successful restaurant for decades is a REAL
accomplishment and the two of you have built something truly special in Rockport.
Your passion, dedication, and the warmth you bring to your guests shine through in
everything you do, and it's an inspiration to all of us in the hospitality industry.

Beyond being amazing restaurateurs, you are also truly wonderful people, and we're
so grateful to know you both. Every time you walk through our doors, you bring such
joy, kindness and friendship, and it truly means the world to us. To celebrate this huge
milestone, we'd love to treat you to a night out on us - please enjoy the enclosed $100
gift card as a small token of our appreciation and admiration.

We hope you take a well-deserved moment to reflect on everything you've
accomplished and to celebrate all the lives you've touched along the way. We're
raising a glass to you both, here's to 25 years of success and many more to come!

With love and admiration,

Jerry Ullman

General Manager
The Double Bull Taphouse

The **DOUBLE BULL**
TAPHOUSE • GRILL

210 Andover St, The Northshore Mall, Unit F100B, Peabody, MA 01970
(978) 817-3670   www.thedoublebull.com

WE DANCE
IN THIS KITCHEN

Nick, Barb, Kathy...

Last night was incredible. We couldn't have asked for a more magical evening and we're so grateful to you for making it happen. The food, the weather, the flowers, the staff, the music, the plane... just WOW. Absolutely unforgettable, and we'll have the photos to prove it soon!

We hope you all got some time to rest and recover. Thank you for all the work you put in to make My Place become Our Place. Your team is amazing and we look forward to many return visits to reminisce and relive the memories.

Michael Mendelsohn or I will stop by tomorrow to pick up the cake board and cake. I think that's all we left behind, but let me know if you stumble upon any other lost treasures!

Love,
Patrick & Teddy

Dearest
Barbara,
I am so
sorry we missed
you. Thank you
for everything.
This is my
favourite
restaurant
in the whole
world.
Love you all!!

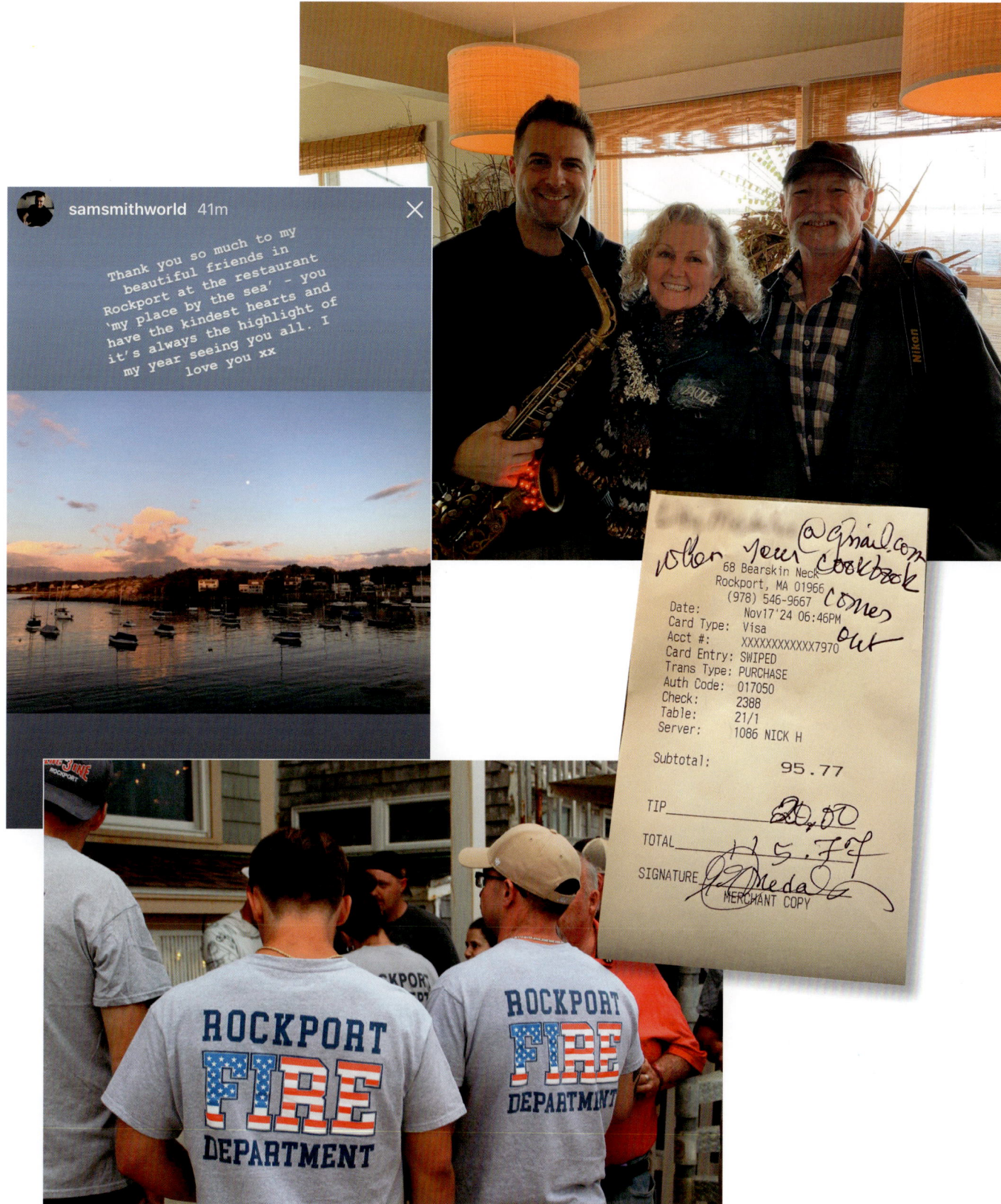

samsmithworld 41m

Thank you so much to my
beautiful friends in
Rockport at the restaurant
'my place by the sea' - you
have the kindest hearts and
it's always the highlight of
my year seeing you all. I
love you all xx

68 Bearskin Neck
Rockport, MA 01966
(978) 546-9667
Date: Nov17'24 06:46PM
Card Type: Visa
Acct #:   XXXXXXXXXXXX7970
Card Entry: SWIPED
Trans Type: PURCHASE
Auth Code: 017050
Check: 2388
Table: 21/1
Server: 1086 NICK H

Subtotal: 95.77

TIP _____   20.00

TOTAL _____   115.77

SIGNATURE _____ Meda

MERCHANT COPY

when your @gmail.com cookbook comes out

My Money's on the Greek!

Ken Novack

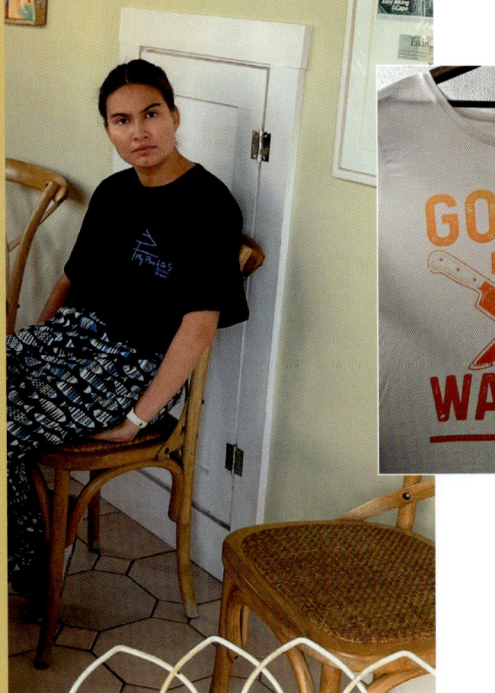

Some places, you have to go, some you want to go

Fishtown Local

Gordon Baird

Every business is different, especially small ones.

The more local they are, the more you tend to keep track of how they did and how you feel afterward. Even if you're just buying a quart of milk or box of Band-Aids, there is that interactive factor, that competence factor, that overworked/understaffed factor. You get a certain taste in your mouth, especially if you go in often. Are they friendly, crabby, funny, slow on the uptakem, do they purposefully avoid your eye when you're in line? Or laugh at your one-liners? Or on their smart phone while trying to work the register? All of the above, right?

Go ahead and hit me with a banana cream pie in the face for daring to venture this opinion — Owner-run businesses just plain run better. Especially when the owners are on premises every day.

Attention, service, attitude, repeat biz, roadblock removal and, most importantly, getting the job done even if that department person isn't on deck.

Businesses like Palazola's Sports in the old days. Closed 10 years ago, yesterday. Jack and Linda were always there to make sure you were taken care of. If the jogging shoe guy was at lunch, Jack himself dug though the shelves for your size. Just like Fred Shrigley at The Rhumbline. If the

trash guy was late, Fred would haul it into the back himself at opening time. It was true for me too with the trash at the West End Theater when they opened the house, or before that at Musician Magazine — if the truck full of magazines arrived at lunch hour, they hadda be unloaded. An owner pitches in and does what is necessary. He/she has skin in the game.

It recently came home going to Rockport's My Place By The Sea for our 46th anniversary. The two partners, Barbara Stavropoulos and Chef Kathy Milbury, have run the place for 26 years in a complete hands-on and "my way" manner. They completely take care of you, going above and beyond, as if they owned the place (!). The same-day-only reservation policy can be aggravating but once there, they treat you so warmly and feed you so well when you are in their house. Barbara will be out there on the floor, shifting tables and chairs and views and fully engaging her guests.

How Sweet It Is to be Loved by You

Desserts

Madow's Tea Party

People often assume the best day ever at My Place by the Sea was the day we bought the restaurant. Wrong! The true best day was when we hosted our niece Madow, her seven friends, and numerous family members for a tea party to celebrate her fourth birthday.

The year before, she chose a "rock n' roll" birthday party theme. About a month before Madow's March 15th birthday, we thought: Wouldn't a tea party at the restaurant be great? When we called her mom, Marissa, she said Madow requested a tea party, so of course, she loved the idea! With a month to prepare, we got busy. And oh, did we prepare!

Barb, given four weeks to plan, was either dangerous or delightfully creative, depending on your perspective. When Madow and her guests arrived at the restaurant, they were greeted outside with a giant flag featuring a photo of Madow in a beautiful dress, and the words, "Happy Birthday, Madow! We love you!!"

Barb and Nick spent hours the night before selecting the perfect Disney soundtrack and transforming the restaurant with balloons, banners, and a light-up neon mirror with the words, "Hello Gorgeous!" Barb pulled out all the stops: a cosmetic table at the entrance with blue lipsticks, unicorn backpacks on rollers, sparkly jewelry, pocketbooks with faces, and oversized hats.

We designed a menu fit for the four-year-olds: tiny tea sandwiches of PB&J and cucumber cream cheese, bite-size cheese quesadillas, mini cream puffs with Valrhona hot fudge, and a teapot-shaped cake made by a local bakery.

When Madow and friends entered the dining room, they found easels and paints set up so they could create artistic masterpieces in between bites of tea sandwiches. We poured tea from whimsical, ceramic rabbit-topped teapots into paper teacups.

After "high tea," the girls took turns at the karaoke machine, and a dance party ensued. Next came the fashion show. We rolled out a red carpet and a catwalk. Once the girls dressed in ballet slippers, jewels, pocketbooks, hats, and makeup, the show began. Our Serbian staff member George, with his deep announcer's voice, introduced each girl as she stepped onto the catwalk while Sly and the Family Stone played "Dance to the Music." Girls who were initially apprehensive and nervous quickly adjusted and enjoyed their moment in the limelight. Blue lipstick, flashy accessories, and big smiles lit up the restaurant.

Nick captured it all in a video set to Disney's "When You Wish Upon a Star." It was unforgettable! Truly, the Best Day Ever!

Coco Daniel

Here's what the *Boston Globe* said about this dessert: "Coco Daniel proved a dessert too tempting to resist (and another dish you won't want to share). The light coconut cake, served on a pool of crème anglaise (a custard sauce), is topped with caramel sauce and sprinkled with chunks of homemade peanut brittle that's good enough to be its own dessert."

The coconut cake recipe came to us from our former baker Daniel, who is originally from Brazil. It was his grandmother's recipe, and over the years, we've made a few small modifications. We still remember sitting on the lower deck of the restaurant, tasting the cake for the first time. Its delicate coconut flavor and tropical feel won us over immediately.

Since then, we've elevated the presentation by serving the cake on a pool of crème anglaise, alongside vanilla gelato, toasted coconut, and during the cooler months, our house-made peanut brittle. At one point, we even paired it with peanut brittle ice cream made from scratch. It's a dessert that brings together creamy, crunchy, salty, and sweet into an irresistible bite.

Coconut cream

Half 15-ounce can coconut milk

Half 15-ounce can Coco Lopez or other brand cream of coconut (shake can to blend before opening)

1 cup half and half

Cake

3 eggs

1 ½ cups granulated sugar

2 tablespoons vanilla extract

1 ½ cups all-purpose flour, plus more for dusting

2 ¼ teaspoons baking powder

¾ cup hot whole milk

Vegetable spray

For serving

Crème Anglaise (see recipe on page 193)

Vanilla gelato

Warm Caramel Sauce (see recipe on page 193)

Toasted coconut

Peanut brittle; only served during colder months

1. Prepare coconut cream:
   In medium bowl, combine all coconut cream ingredients and set aside.

2. Mix cake:
   Preheat oven to 350 degrees and set to convection if available. Spray 9-inch by 13-inch metal or glass pan with vegetable spray and dust with flour. In stand mixer, or using hand mixer, whisk the eggs, sugar, and vanilla for 5 minutes until pale yellow. With mixer running on low, add flour and baking powder, then slowly pour in hot milk, scraping the bowl to mix well.

3. Bake cake:
Pour batter into pan and bake until cake tester or knife comes out clean, about 18 minutes, depending on your oven. Remove cake and immediately poke holes all over the cake, using a fork to pierce holes through to the cake bottom. Pour coconut cream over cake. Once cake is cool, if you are not serving it right away, store in refrigerator.

4. Plate cake:
Using a 3-inch diameter round cookie cutter, cut cake circles. Spoon crème anglaise on the center of each plate and top with one cake circle. Spoon a dollop of vanilla gelato on the cake, drizzle with warm caramel sauce, and sprinkle with toasted coconut and peanut brittle (if using).

MAKES 9-INCH BY 13-INCH CAKE OR ABOUT 8 SERVINGS WHEN CUT INTO 3-INCH ROUNDS

Apple Tarts

Make these and your guests will proclaim you a dessert hero! Serve the tarts warm with vanilla or cinnamon gelato and garnish with fresh mint. This recipe is the epitome of the My Place philosophy: simple, delicious, and letting the food speak for itself.

4 Granny Smith apples, peeled, cored, and cut into ¼-inch slices

1 teaspoon cinnamon

1 cup granulated sugar

1 puff pastry sheet thawed overnight in refrigerator (keep in the refrigerator until ready to use)

½ cup melted unsalted butter

For serving

Gelato

Mint sprigs

Caramel Sauce (see recipe on page 193)

1. Prepare apples:
   Preheat oven to 400 degrees. In medium bowl, combine apples with cinnamon and sugar. Line rimmed baking sheet with parchment or foil. Place apples in four piles on baking sheet, ensuring piles have space around them.

2. Prepare puff pastry:
   Place puff pastry sheet on flat surface. Using small (5- or 6-inch diameter) plate as a guide, cut four circles with a knife. Stretch circles to cover apple piles and place over apples. Alternatively, cut pastry into squares. Brush tops with melted butter.

3. Bake tarts:
   Bake until pastry tops are golden brown and crispy, about 30 minutes.

4. Serve warm with gelato, Caramel Sauce, and mint sprigs.

SERVES 4

The Whirlwind Birthday Surprise

On my birthday one year, Barb said let's take the day off. "We'll go to the beach, then go to dinner." That sounded perfect to me. When we returned from the beach, Barb said, "Do you want to drive, or should we let him?" Just then, a car pulled up.

Once we were on the road, I didn't know where we were going. Barb handed me a wrapped gift... a snow globe of New York City. What's going on— are we driving to New York? I thought. No, but I soon realized that we were headed to Boston's Logan Airport!

When the car pulled up to the departures area, Barb grinned and revealed, "We have a reservation at Vong, in New York City!" Are you serious?! One of my culinary heroes is Jean-Georges Vongerichten, and the thought of dining at his innovative French-Thai restaurant was more than thrilling.

When we arrived at the airport gate, I realized I didn't have my driver's license, or any form of ID. Smiling at the gate attendant, I explained: "It's my birthday, this trip was a surprise, and I don't have my ID."

I pleaded with the man and told him my brother Mike is the GM of the New York Islanders. "He flies this route all the time and you've probably seen him," I said. "Just look at me. I'm sure you can tell that we're related." He studied my face, nodded, and sure enough, he allowed me to board the plane!

Mike had arranged for us to be picked up at New York's LaGuardia Airport and taken to Vong. Dinner was spectacular! Afterward, the same car returned us to the airport, and I managed to get on another flight without my ID. By 11 p.m. we were back to close the restaurant in Rockport. To this day, Barb and I smile every time we think about that night. It was like a crazy, wonderful dream.

—Kath

Chocolate Tasting

This combination dessert is a tribute to four chefs Kathy admires. The Warm-Cool Chocolate is a nod to Jacques and Laurent Pourcel, French twin brothers who created the Michelin three-star restaurant Le Jardin des Sens in Montpellier. Something Chocolate, which we like to pair with Marianne's Hot Fudge, is a variation of Wolfgang Puck's Best-Ever Chocolate Cake.

The Chocolate Soufflé has a fun backstory. Jean-Georges Vongerichten, one of Kath's favorite chefs and an ongoing source of inspiration, introduced molten chocolate cake. But the funny thing about molten chocolate cake is that it was a complete accident; one of Jean-Georges' cooks, under pressure to serve a large party, removed a batch of cakes from the oven too soon. The cake interior was molten, which, as it turned out, everyone loved.

As fate would have it, at My Place, our Chocolate Soufflé was created by complete accident, too. One of the cooks thought our cake batter was hot fudge and placed it in the microwave to warm it. It bubbled up over the sides of the container and made what turned out to be a delicious souffle! We finish the soufflé with crème anglaise poured into the center.

Warm-Cool Chocolate

Chocolate Ganache (see recipe on page 191)

Whipped Cream (recipe below)

Espresso Granita (recipe below; use half for this recipe)

In 3-ounce shot glasses, fill with ⅓ warmed chocolate ganache, ⅓ whipped cream, and ⅓ espresso granita. Serve immediately.

SERVES 6

Espresso Granita

1 cup cold espresso or iced coffee

¼ cup **Simple Syrup** (see recipe below)

1 tablespoon Kahlua (optional)

Combine all ingredients in a small bowl. Pour mixture into a shallow metal or glass baking dish and place in freezer.

After 30 minutes, use fork to scrape and break up any large ice chunks. Return to freezer. Continue scraping and stirring every 30 minutes for about 2 to 3 hours, or until mixture has light, fluffy, crystalline texture.

MAKES 2 SERVINGS

Whipped Cream

1 cup heavy cream

1 tablespoon vanilla extract

1 teaspoon granulated sugar

Combine all ingredients and whip until stiff peaks form. Chill until ready to serve.

Simple Syrup

In saucepan over medium-high heat, bring equal parts water and sugar to a boil. Let cool before using in recipe.

Chocolate Soufflés

3 whole eggs

2 egg yolks

1 tablespoon vanilla extract

½ cup granulated sugar

5 tablespoons flour

1 stick (4 ounces) unsalted butter

¾ cup chocolate chips

Garnish: **Crème Anglaise** (see recipe on page 193)

1. Mix batter:
   In medium-size bowl, whisk eggs and vanilla until well blended. Whisk in sugar, then blend in flour. In separate microwave-safe bowl, melt butter and chocolate, about 1 ½ minutes. Stir well, heating for additional time if mixture has lumps. Combine chocolate and egg mixtures, stir well, and pour batter into six 2-ounce, small microwave-safe ramekins.

2. Bake soufflés:
   Put ramekins in microwave 35-40 seconds or until the soufflé puffs up above the ramekin top. Remove from microwave, cut an X in the soufflé top, and pour in 1 tablespoon crème anglaise!

SERVES 6

Something Chocolate

You might think that 5 tablespoons of vanilla is a lot, but it isn't. Our recipe tester skimped on the vanilla, using only 3 tablespoons, and when Kathy tasted the test cake, she immediately detected that it was missing the full quantity of vanilla. Use real vanilla and use the full 5 tablespoons!

2 ¼ cups granulated sugar, divided

1 ½ cups all-purpose flour

1 ⅛ cups cocoa (we use Valrhona)

1 ½ teaspoons baking powder

½ teaspoon kosher salt

6 eggs, separated

3 egg whites

¾ cup water

1 ¼ cups vegetable oil

5 tablespoons vanilla

1. Preheat oven to 350 degrees. Spray 9-inch by 13-inch cake pan with vegetable spray and line with parchment paper. Dust with flour.

2. In medium-size bowl, sift together 1 ¼ cup sugar, flour, cocoa, baking powder, and salt. In large bowl combine 6 egg yolks, water, oil, and vanilla, then mix in dry ingredients.

3. Add 9 egg whites to large mixing bowl. Using a handheld mixer or stand mixer, whip egg whites, while slowly adding 1 cup sugar, and continue beating until stiff peaks form. Gently fold egg white and sugar mixture into batter.

4. Pour batter into pan and tap to distribute evenly. Bake 30-35 minutes, until knife pierces cake cleanly. Do not overbake!

To serve Chocolate Tasting: On each serving plate, place: Warm-Cool Chocolate in shot glass, Chocolate Soufflé with crème anglaise, a square of Something Chocolate, and extra crème anglaise in a small container.

SERVES 12 AND MAKES ONE 9-INCH BY 13-INCH CAKE

Chocolate Ganache

Silky and rich, this chocolate ganache is the ultimate finishing touch. It's surprisingly simple to make with just five ingredients. We use it to fill pastry for Chocolate Purses (see page 199), and it's part of our Warm-Cool Chocolate (see page 188). It's also a decadent ice cream and cake topping.

½ cup heavy cream

1 tablespoon unsalted butter

1 tablespoon granulated sugar

6 ounces high-quality semisweet or bittersweet chocolate

1 tablespoon vanilla extract

Place all ingredients in microwave-safe bowl. Heat for 1 minute, stir, and repeat heating and stirring until sauce is smooth. Chill in refrigerator for at least 30 minutes or until ready to serve.

Marianne's Hot Fudge Sauce

Marianne Novack was an elegant, smart, and loving person with a delightful, clever sense of humor. We loved her and we miss her every day. We named this Marianne's Hot Fudge Sauce because it was her favorite. This recipe was originally given to us by Dodie, our favorite Sid Wainer produce gal.

¾ cup whole milk

¾ cup heavy cream

2 tablespoons plus 2 teaspoons butter

2 tablespoons plus 2 teaspoons margarine

⅔ cup brown sugar

⅔ cup granulated sugar

1 ½ teaspoons vanilla extract

1 cup unsweetened cocoa powder (we prefer Valrhona)

1. In a large saucepan over medium-high heat, combine all ingredients except cocoa, stirring constantly until butter and margarine are melted. Reduce heat to low, add cocoa, and stir to combine, about 2 minutes.

2. Remove from heat. Use a whisk or handheld blender to remove lumps.

Crème Anglaise

We love this traditional English custard sauce as an accompaniment to many desserts.

4 egg yolks

½ cup granulated sugar

1 ½ cups heavy cream

3 tablespoons vanilla

1. Fill a large bowl with equal amounts of ice and cold water and set aside.

   In medium-size bowl, whisk egg yolks and sugar to combine. Combine cream and vanilla in medium saucepan over medium heat. It should be hot but not boiling.

2. Slowly add about ½ cup of the hot cream to the egg mixture to temper it. Then slowly add egg and sugar mixture to saucepan. Keep on medium heat, whisking constantly, until it thickens enough that when you dip a spoon in it and run your finger over the spoon it leaves a clean trail.

3. Pour hot crème anglaise into a separate container that will fit in the ice bath to chill. Whisk while sauce is cooling in ice bath. Use immediately or refrigerate until ready to use.

MAKES ABOUT 2 CUPS

Caramel Sauce

1 ½ cups sugar

½ cup water

3 tablespoons unsalted butter cut into pieces

1 cup heavy cream

2 teaspoons vanilla extract

In medium-size saucepan, add water and sugar and heat over medium-high until golden brown without stirring. Reduce heat to low to avoid spattering, then carefully whisk in butter a little at a time. Slowly add cream, whisking constantly, then add vanilla and whisk until combined and smooth. Remove from heat and serve warm.

MAKES ABOUT 1½ CUPS

Strawberry Shortcake

This classic dessert is a fan favorite. Layers of tender, lemon-scented cake, macerated strawberries, and lightly sweetened whipped cream come together for an elegant treat. Cut the cake into rounds or squares, slice them horizontally to produce two layers, and stack with strawberries and whipped cream filling for a WOW presentation. Garnish with fresh mint for a standout dessert!

Strawberry topping

1 pound sliced strawberries

½ cup granulated sugar

Grated lemon rind from half a lemon

Cake

3 eggs

1 ½ cups granulated sugar

1 teaspoon vanilla

1 ½ cups all-purpose flour, plus more for dusting

2 ¼ teaspoons baking powder

¾ cup hot milk

1 teaspoon lemon zest

Juice of 1 ½ lemons

Whipped Cream (see recipe on page 188, double recipe)

Garnish: Fresh mint

1. Prepare strawberries:
   Mix strawberries, sugar, and lemon rind in large bowl. Cover with plastic and let sit in warm area until strawberries have softened and become saucy, at least 1 hour.

2. Prepare cake:
   Preheat oven to 350 degrees and set to convection if possible. In stand mixer or using hand mixer, whip eggs, sugar, and vanilla for 5 minutes until pale yellow. Add flour and baking powder, slowly pour in hot milk, and mix at low speed. Mix in lemon zest and juice.

   Spray 9-inch by 13-inch pan with vegetable spray and dust with flour. Pour batter into pan and bake until cake tester or knife comes out clean, about 18 minutes. Remove from oven to cool.

3. Assemble individual cakes:
   We like to use a round cookie cutter, about 5 inches in diameter, to cut circles (see note below). You also can cut the cake into 8 rectangles or squares. Cut each circle or rectangle in half horizontally so you have two layers of cake. Place cake on each plate, top with strawberries and their juice, whipped cream, another cake layer, strawberries, and whipped cream. Garnish with fresh mint.

Note: If you cut cake circles, make parfaits with the excess cake trimmings! Place in parfait glasses or bowls along with whipped cream and berries.

SERVES 6-8

Lemon Tart

We love this refreshing dessert as the perfect finish for a seafood meal.

1 ⅓ cups graham cracker crumbs

⅓ cup melted unsalted butter

3 tablespoons granulated sugar

1 14-ounce can sweetened condensed milk

¾ cup fresh-squeezed lemon juice, from 4-5 lemons
(do not use bottled lemon juice)

4 egg yolks

4 teaspoons lemon zest

Garnish: Whipped cream and fresh berries

1. Prepare crust:
   Preheat oven to 350 degrees. In large mixing bowl, combine graham cracker crumbs, melted butter, and sugar, and mix well. Spread graham cracker crust on bottom of 8- by 8-inch pan evenly, pressing it down with your fingertips (crust is only on the bottom). Bake until golden brown, about 7 minutes. Let crust cool, then chill in refrigerator for 30 minutes. Crust can be prepared a day or two in advance.

2. While crust is chilling, prepare lemon filling:
   Keep oven at 350 degrees. In bowl of electric stand mixer or using a handheld mixer, combine condensed milk, lemon juice, egg yolks, and lemon zest, and mix until pale yellow and fluffy.

3. Pour filling evenly into crust, and tap pan against counter to ensure filling is spread evenly. Bake until edges are firm but there's a bit of movement in tart's center, about 8-15 minutes. Let tart cool and refrigerate; tart will continue to firm up as it cools. Serve cold with whipped cream and berries of your choice.

SERVES 9 AND MAKES AN 8-INCH BY 8-INCH DESSERT

Apple Crunch

This classic apple crunch is everything an apple dessert should be: cozy, comforting, and full of rich flavor and texture. As it bakes, it fills your kitchen with the fragrant aroma of cinnamon and apples. Tart Granny Smiths are tossed with sugar and spice, then topped with a golden, buttery mix of oats, brown sugar, and three kinds of chopped nuts for extra crunch and depth. It's easy to make ahead and perfect for feeding a crowd. We love serving it warm with a scoop of vanilla or cinnamon ice cream and a drizzle of caramel sauce.

During Rockport festivals, Daniel, our baker, and Kath would donate this dish to raise funds for the festival committee. We would be accosted by locals asking, "Is that the Apple Crunch?" and, "How do you get your topping so crunchy?"

Topping

1 ½ cups rolled oats (not instant or steel cut)

½ cup all-purpose flour

½ cup packed brown sugar

1 ⅓ sticks (12 tablespoons) unsalted butter, at room temperature

¼ cup chopped walnuts

¼ cup chopped pecans

¼ cup blanched, chopped almonds

1 ½ teaspoons cinnamon

½ teaspoon kosher salt

Apple mixture

10 Granny Smith apples, peeled, cored, and cut into ⅛-inch or ¼-inch slices

1 cup granulated sugar

1 tablespoon cinnamon

Optional accompaniments: Ice cream and **Caramel Sauce** (see recipe on page 193)

1. Prepare topping:
   Preheat oven to 450 degrees. In large bowl, combine all topping ingredients until well mixed.

2. Mix apples and bake:
   In another large bowl, combine apples with sugar and cinnamon. Pour apples into 9-inch by 13-inch baking pan. Sprinkle topping over apples.

3. Cover with aluminum foil and bake 1 hour. Remove foil. The sugar should be caramelized and bubbling. Reduce oven to 350 degrees and return the pan to oven to brown the top. Check after 5 minutes. Cool slightly and serve warm or room temperature with ice cream and Caramel Sauce.

MAKES 12 SERVINGS (9-INCH BY 13-INCH PAN)

Prickly Pear Champagne Granita

This light dessert is a delightful, slightly sweet finish to a meal. It's also a perfect use of leftover champagne (if such a thing exists!). Serve over fresh berries for a light summer dessert.

2 cups champagne

¼ cup prickly pear purée, or other fruit puree of your choice

⅓ cup **Simple Syrup** (see recipe on page 188)

1. Combine all ingredients in a small bowl. Pour mixture into a shallow metal or glass baking dish and place in freezer.

2. After 30 minutes, use fork to scrape and break up any large ice chunks. Return to freezer. Continue scraping and stirring every 30 minutes for about 2 to 3 hours, or until entire mixture has a light, fluffy, crystalline texture.

SERVES 4

Almond Joy

This crowd-pleasing dessert features elegant little "purses"—crisp, buttery puff pastry that encloses chilled chocolate ganache, which melts into a molten surprise once baked. They're indulgent on their own, and become a memorable dessert when paired with coconut chocolate chip ice cream, toasted coconut, almonds, a drizzle of hot fudge sauce, and a dollop of whipped cream. Best of all, you can assemble the purses ahead of time and bake them just before serving. It's an impressive dinner party dessert that's surprisingly simple to make at home.

This recipe calls for half a sheet of puff pastry, but you'll need to thaw a full sheet to prepare it. We suggest making an extra batch of chocolate purses and freezing them for a ready-made dessert.

Chocolate purses

Chocolate Ganache (see recipe on page 191), chilled until solid (important for forming the purses)

½ sheet frozen puff pastry, thawed overnight in refrigerator

1 ½ sticks (12 tablespoons) melted unsalted butter or 6 ounces ghee (clarified butter)

Accompaniments

6 scoops coconut chocolate chip ice cream or other ice cream of your choice

6 tablespoons toasted coconut flakes

1 ½ cups warmed **Marianne's Hot Fudge Sauce** (see recipe on page 192)

6 tablespoons toasted almonds

Garnish: Whipped cream

1. Make Chocolate Ganache (see recipe on page 191) and chill until solid.

2. Form purses:
   Preheat oven to 425 degrees. Roll pastry out to ¹/₈-inch thickness and cut puff pastry into 12 squares measuring 2 ½ inches by 2 ½ inches. Spoon 1 tablespoon of chilled chocolate ganache onto the center of each pastry square. Pull the sides up one corner at a time, pinch just below the top to close it, twist, and fold each flap over so each tip looks like a flower petal.

3. Place purses on rimmed baking sheet and drizzle with butter. Bake until golden brown, about 6 minutes.

4. Plate desserts:
   On each plate, place two warm chocolate purses, ½ tablespoon toasted coconut, and one scoop of ice cream. Sprinkle remaining coconut and toasted almonds over the plates. Garnish with hot fudge sauce—we like serving it in decorative shot glasses—and a dollop of whipped cream.

SERVES 6

Index

"Oh Deer.
  I think that's Sam's purse!!!"

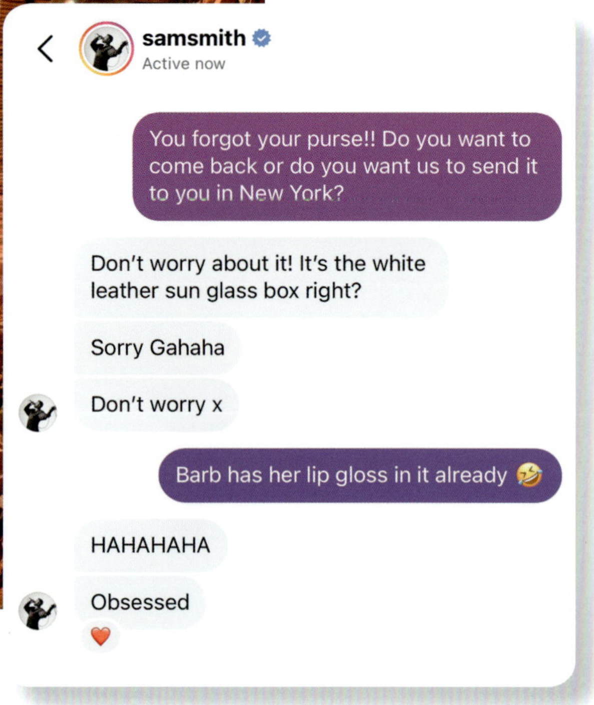

samsmith ✓
Active now

You forgot your purse!! Do you want to come back or do you want us to send it to you in New York?

Don't worry about it! It's the white leather sun glass box right?

Sorry Gahaha

Don't worry x

Barb has her lip gloss in it already 🤣

HAHAHAHA

Obsessed
❤️